Pasta Tecnica

Pasquale Bruno, Jr.

CONTEMPORARY
BOOKS, INC.
CHICAGO

Library of Congress Cataloging in Publication Data

Bruno, Pasquale.
    Pasta tecnica.

    Includes index.
    1. Cookery (Macaroni)   I. Title.
TX809.M17B78   1981   641.8'22   81-65187
ISBN 0-8092-5895-1   AACR2
ISBN 0-8092-5894-3 (pbk.)

Photographs by Donald Link

Copyright © 1982, 1981 by Pasquale Bruno, Jr.
All rights reserved
Published by Contemporary Books, Inc.
180 North Michigan Avenue, Chicago, Illinois 60601
Manufactured in the United States of America
Library of Congress Catalog Card Number: 81-65187
International Standard Book Number: 0-8092-5895-1 (cloth)
                                    0-8092-5894-3 (paper)

Published simultaneously in Canada by
Beaverbooks, Ltd.
150 Lesmill Road
Don Mills, Ontario M3B 2T5
Canada

Contents

Introduction

I have been looking at pasta in one form or another since the time that my eyes were level with the table in my mother's kitchen—and a big kitchen it is. It had to be large to make enough homemade pasta to satisfy my father and my three brothers, plus uncles, aunts, and cousins who used to happen by just to say hello but seemed to linger just long enough to sample a plate of pasta. At a recent gathering of the clan I counted twenty-three serious eaters around a table laden with Italian food. The recipes—if they existed, for my mother never uses them—would make a first-rate Italian cookbook.

Some of the dishes in this book come from on-the-job learning in my mother's kitchen. Some are creations of my own. Some are variations of classical Italian dishes, and they are variations only insofar as certain substitutions made for ingredients available only in Italy.

Many books on Italian cooking have crossed and crisscrossed the paths and tracings of the origins of pasta. This book will make no attempt to do so. This is a *cookbook*, not a history book, and it is intended to help you create an array of pasta dishes that are truly enjoyable.

There are boundaries that dictate the regional variations of the pasta of Italy. These barriers need not exist in your kitchen. The red sauces of southern Italy can surely be coupled with the "pasta of the North," and the butter and cream sauces of the North can be wed with the "pasta of the South."

A great deal of local pride is mixed into each recipe from the many provinces of Italy. To the cooks in those provinces their way of cooking a particular dish is the authentic and only way, and any change is deception. I do not feel bound by those local restrictions. We shall explore variations and combinations with which some severe purists might not agree. The most important thing is the end result and the tingle to your palate. The essential aspects of any type of cooking are the ingredients used, preparation, logical order, and attention to detail. This book will cover all those factors, and if you follow them you will have no problems in making and serving pasta dishes that will delight you and please you. To me, that is a most pleasant thought.

1

Pasta-Making Equipment

You don't need a kitchen full of machines, tools, and gadgets to make pasta, but some items can save time and work.

The pasta machine is one item that is almost indispensable. The machine shown here is the Atlas, made in Italy. It does an excellent job of rolling the dough and cutting it. It comes with two cutting heads—one for making fettuccine and one for the narrower tagliarini—and a clamp for attaching the machine to the counter. The cutting head is removable and additional cutting heads are available for cutting different types of pasta. The two extra heads shown here are for cutting spaghetti and lasagna.

If you wish to move things along a little faster, try an electric pasta machine like the Bialetti model shown here. It rolls and cuts the dough in the same fashion as the manual machine, and the cutters that come with the machine make the same kind of pasta. No extra cutting heads are available as of this writing. The machine is a bit noisy and usually retails for something over $100. In spite of all this, the Bialetti does work well.

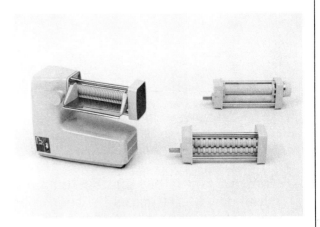

Shown next are three pasta cutters. The one on the left can be used to cut and seal ravioli. The one in the center does the same but much more effectively and is known as a Krimp-Cut Sealer. The cutter on the right is a *duplex cutter*. The wavy-edged wheel can be used to make a wavy rim on noodles for lasagna or papparadelle; the smooth-edged wheel is excellent for cutting strips of pasta, evening up sheets of dough, cutting squares for cannelloni, and so forth.

Here are two of several different types of forms for making ravioli. Both do an excellent job of cutting and sealing filled ravioli. Note that it is possible to make twelve ravioli at a time. One company makes a similar version that makes ten quite large ravioli. How they are used is shown in the ravioli section of Chapter 7.

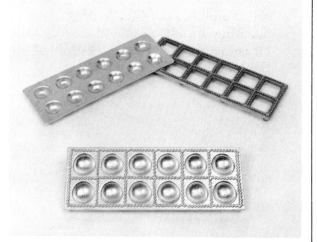

Next are two rolling pins for thinning pasta dough. The one on the right is an authentic pasta pin that allows you to roll the pasta dough around the circumference of the pin for maximum hand pressure. It is approximately 30 inches long and 1½ inches in diameter. The one on the right is a ball bearing pin that does an equally good job of thinning the dough. Take your pick.

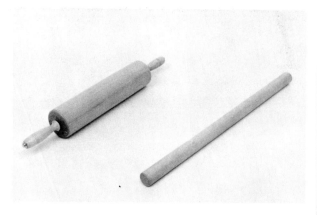

A dough scraper is a useful tool, especially if you mix your dough on a countertop or pastry board.

This pot, called a spaghetti cooker, is perfect for cooking all types of pasta. The removable colander works especially well for draining delicate pasta like ravioli. The eight-quart size allows for plenty of room to cook a pound or more of pasta.

This is an excellent machine for making cavatelli (also known as seashells and gnocchi). A tube-shaped piece of fresh dough is fed between the two wheels on the right while a crank is turned and the pieces are rolled and cut automatically. It will be shown in use in the recipe chapters.

This is called a Pasta-lift. It is probably the best device ever made for scooping pasta out of water. It is made of stainless steel and will last a lifetime.

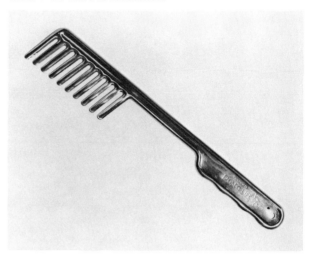

NOTE: You will see a food mill being used in many of the recipes. If you don't have one, chop the tomatoes in the can with a knife before using. A food processor or blender should not be used as a substitute, as they tend to homogenize the tomatoes.

This is a pasta drying rack. Cut pasta is hung over the dowel arms for drying. The large vertical dowel can be removed from the base so that all the pasta can be taken directly to the pot for cooking.

Basic Ingredients

Flour

The flour to be used is *all-purpose, unbleached.* Unbleached flour has a very high gluten content that delivers a firm pasta dough. It is not necessary to sift the flour for the recipes in this book. Follow the dip-and-sweep method described later.

Tomatoes

Fresh vine-ripened plum tomatoes would always be the first choice for the start of an excellent tomato sauce. However, the availability and seasonal nature of plum tomatoes work against us. Canned Italian-style plum tomatoes are a close second and highly recommended for all red sauces. I have found that tomatoes packed in California are of comparable quality to the Italian imports—and a lot less expensive.

Tomato Paste

Buy paste in the tube if you can in order to avoid waste. Tomato paste should be used sparingly since its concentrated flavor goes a long way. In many recipes I find it essential to improve a sauce that might lack the necessary tomato flavor. This is particularly likely to be the case when the tomatoes you have were canned before they were fully ripened.

Olive Oil

Only the purest first-pressing oils should be used in Italian cooking. Extra-virgin oil is dark green and tastes light and fruity.

Prosciutto

Prosciutto has many variations. The kind you want is prosciutto crudo (raw prosciutto). It is readily available in this country and is quite good, though not as good as that found in Italy. It is perfectly acceptable for recipes calling for this delicious unsmoked ham.

Cream

The cream called for in the recipes in this book is heavy whipping cream (not half and half).

Parmesan Cheese

Use only freshly grated Parmesan—imported or domestic. If you can afford it, use the imported cheese because there is a difference in the richness of the taste. Grate as much as you need from the wedge just before using, if possible. Store the unused portion of the wedge in the refrigerator, wrapped in plastic wrap and foil. This will prevent it from drying out too quickly. Never use cheese sold in bottles or containers that is already grated. It is bland and salty and bears no resemblance to real Parmesan. The same holds true for Romano cheese.

Ricotta

Real whole-milk ricotta is not available in this country. I have found, however, that the ricotta that is available works very well. Do not substitute cottage cheese for any reason.

Ingredients basic to certain dishes will be discussed in the individual recipes.

Using Fresh Tomatoes

There is only one time when it is preferable to use fresh tomatoes and not the canned ones—during the peak of the tomato growing season, when tomatoes are fresh, vine-ripened, and flavorful. If you are growing your own tomatoes, by all means use them, especially if you are growing in your garden the Burpee, Roma VF, or San Marzano types of plum tomatoes. These will give you an excellent red sauce.

You will need about 2 to 2½ pounds of tomatoes in place of the large (28-ounce) can of tomatoes recommended for the recipes in this book.

When using fresh tomatoes, follow this method for peeling and seeding:

1   Use firm ripe tomatoes. Slide the tomatoes, one or two at a time, into boiling water and boil for ten seconds. Remove from the water at once.

2   Cut out the stem.

3   Peel off the skin, working out from the stem hole.

4   Cut the tomato in half crosswise. Do this over a strainer, placed in a pan, to collect the extra juice.

5   Gently squeeze each half to remove the
seeds. Use your fingers to finish the job.

Chop the tomatoes and use in a sauce as
you would the canned tomatoes.

The method is the same for plum tomatoes
except they are cut lengthwise.

*Each year my mother processes fresh
tomatoes from my father's garden into
tomato puree for canning. She usually
makes between 100 and 150 quarts for use
throughout the year.*

3

Making Pasta Dough by Hand

Basic Pasta Dough

¾ cup all-purpose
   unbleached flour
1 extra-large egg

These are the only two ingredients you need to make an excellent pasta dough. It may be necessary on occasion to add a bit of warm water to form a workable dough if the liquid content of the egg is low or the absorption balance of the flour is high.

To increase the serving portions, increase the egg and flour in equal quantities—1½ cups of flour and 2 extra-large eggs, for example. The basic recipe will make enough dough for approximately 7 to 8 ounces of pasta noodles. For stuffed pasta, such as ravioli and layered pasta like lasagna, follow the individual recipes for the proper amount.

1   Use the dip-and-sweep method for measuring the flour. Dip the measuring cup into the flour and sweep it off with the straight edge of a knife.

2 Form a well with a knife or your fingers to hold the eggs. Keep the sides high to prevent the eggs from running out of the well.

3 Drop the eggs into the center of the well.

4 Scramble the eggs with a fork and start to pick up the flour from inside the well with the fork, incorporating the flour into the eggs gradually until the eggs are no longer runny.

5 At this point you must use your hands. Bring all the flour from the outside of the well into the center.

6 Form the entire mass into a ball. Use the excess flour outside the ball only if the dough feels wet. In that case, bring it in gradually as needed to form a soft but not sticky ball of dough.

7 Pick up the ball of dough and squeeze it firmly between your hands while rotating it.

8   Now begin the kneading process. Push down on the dough firmly, with the heel of your hand pushing into the center of the dough.

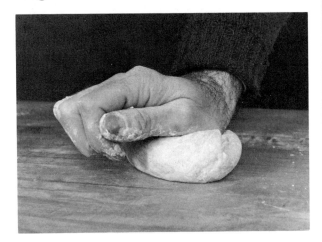

9   Give the dough quarter turns while you are kneading. If the dough sticks to your hand, dust it with flour and continue kneading. A 2-egg recipe generally requires 8 to 10 minutes of kneading.

10   Your objective is to finish with a ball of dough that is smooth and satiny but not tough.

If you have had experience in making any kind of dough using flour, you should have no trouble. If not, don't despair if you don't succeed the first time around. It's a very simple process and you will get the hang of it quickly. It is important to remember, if the dough feels at all sticky to the hand, to dust it lightly with flour but not to use more flour than is necessary.

Basic Pasta Dough— Pasta Verde (Green Noodles)

The technique for making green noodles is the same as that used for *Basic Pasta Dough.* The only difference is the addition of spinach.

1   Use 1½ cups of flour, 2 large eggs, and one-half of a 10-ounce package of frozen chopped spinach. Cook the spinach according to package directions, drain well, and cool. Squeeze as much water out of the spinach as you can, then squeeze again. Chop the spinach finely. The photo shows about how much spinach you need.

2   Add the spinach to the eggs in the well of flour, incorporating it into eggs.

3   Bring the flour into the eggs and spinach from inside the well.

4   Continue incorporating the eggs, flour, and spinach until you have used practically all the flour.

5   Now squeeze the entire mass into a ball with your hands. Scrape away the excess flour.

6   Knead the dough by hand for 8 to 10 minutes. Add additional flour as needed. Spinach pasta absorbs a great deal of flour.

4

Making Pasta Dough in the Food Processor

Basic Pasta Dough

The food processor is a most convenient tool for making pasta dough. The basic characteristics of the finished dough are slightly altered from the handmade type in that the dough is softer. This is an advantage since the dough is easier to work with during the rolling process.

1   Use the steel blade when making dough for pasta. Put the flour and the eggs into the work bowl. Start the machine and let it run for about 30 seconds.

2   If the eggs were not liquid enough, or if too much flour was used, the dough will not ball up and will look like this.

3   To get the dough to ball up, add a small quantity of warm water through the feed tube while the machine is running. Use a light hand as you will need only a small amount of water.

4   If you add too much water, the dough will ball up but will be too moist and parts of the dough will stick to the sides of the work bowl, as shown.

5   In that case, add a bit of flour directly into the work bowl and turn on the machine.

6   Let the machine run for 30 to 45 seconds. This will finish the actual kneading of the dough. Notice that the dough has formed a ball and the sides of the work bowl are free of any excess dough.

After you have made 2 or 3 batches of pasta dough in the processor you will no doubt find it unnecessary to add additional water or flour to get the dough to ball up. When

you retrieve the finished dough from the work bowl it may feel a bit moist. Dust it with flour and knead it for a few seconds by hand. No further kneading is necessary before hand or machine rolling.

Spinach Pasta Dough

1   Use the steel blade. Add the flour and the cooked and well-drained spinach to the work bowl. Start the machine and let it run for about 10 seconds. This will chop the spinach and incorporate it into the flour.

2   Add the eggs to the work bowl. Start the machine and let it run for about 30 seconds.

3   The dough will ball, but it will be very moist because of the water in the spinach. Add flour, about a tablespoon at a time, through the feed tube, keeping the machine running constantly, until you have a solid ball of dough and none of the dough is sticking to the sides of the work bowl.

The more moisture you squeeze out of the cooked spinach at the start, the less additional flour you will need to add to form a workable ball of spinach dough. As you add flour through the feed tube the dough will break apart. When the flour is incorporated, a ball will re-form. Check the dough often. If it feels sticky, add another dose of flour. After removing the dough from the work bowl, dust it with flour and knead it for about 1 minute by hand. It should now be ready for hand or machine rolling.

5

Basic Pasta Dough

Manual, or hand-cranked, pasta machines generally have a set of rollers for kneading and thinning the dough and a set of cutters for cutting the sheet of dough into noodles. I recommend two machines most highly—the Atlas and the Imperia. Each of these machines comes with a set of cutting heads that will cut perfect fettuccine noodles and the narrower tagliarini noodles. The cutting head on both of these machines is removable and can be replaced by optional cutting heads for making spaghetti, lasagna, papparadelle, trenette, and so forth. A good cookware specialty store can advise you of the optional cutters available for each machine. Needless to say, a pasta machine is a great time saver. If you are a pasta lover, it's almost an absolute necessity.

1   Once you have formed a ball of dough, as shown earlier—by hand or with a food processor—cut the ball into a number of pieces equal to the number of eggs used. Cover all but one piece with a damp paper towel or a clean dish towel to prevent it from drying out. With the rollers at their widest setting—#1 on the Atlas, #0 on the Imperia—feed a piece of dough into the rollers while turning the handle. The dough will flatten out.

2   Fold the dough into thirds.

3   Press it down firmly at the seam.

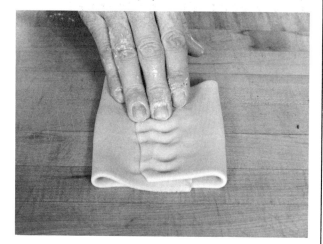

4   Feed it through the rollers again. Repeat the folding and pressing and feed through the rollers. Do this 6 to 8 times or until the dough feels smooth and satiny. If at any time the dough feels sticky, dust it with flour.

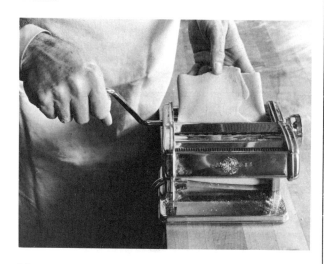

5   Now you are ready to thin out the dough. Decrease the space between the rollers by one notch. Feed the sheet of dough through the rollers again. At this point you no longer fold the dough into thirds.

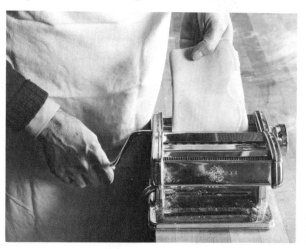

6   Decrease the space between the rollers one more notch and feed the dough through again.

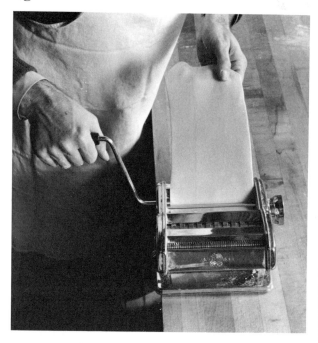

7   Notice the consistency of the dough—smooth and satiny. Continue to decrease the space between the rollers one notch at a time while feeding the dough through the rollers. If the dough feels the least bit sticky, dust both sides with flour.

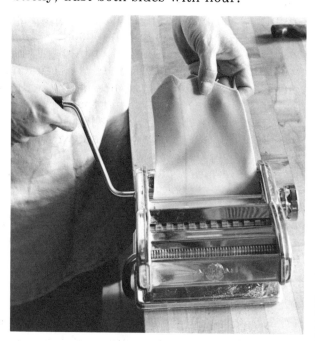

8   Notice how the dough is stretching and thinning. If the sheet of dough is getting too long to be manageable, cut it in half crosswise. The last roller setting on most manual machines makes the pasta extremely thin. You may find it to your liking to stop at the next-to-the-last setting

or, if you like your pasta a little thicker, two settings from the end. You have to be the judge of this.

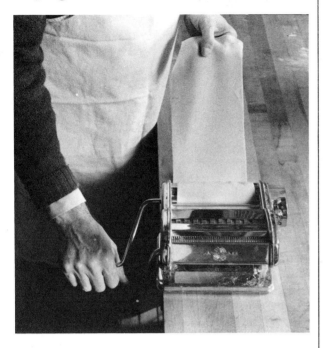

In the classes that I teach on pasta making, the single biggest mistake students make is failing to dust the dough with flour when necessary. Always follow this simple rule: If the dough feels the least bit sticky, dust it with flour. If you remember this, you will have no problems in making the very best pasta dough. Now on to the cutting.

9 If you wish to cut fettuccine noodles, feed the sheet of dough through the wider cutters.

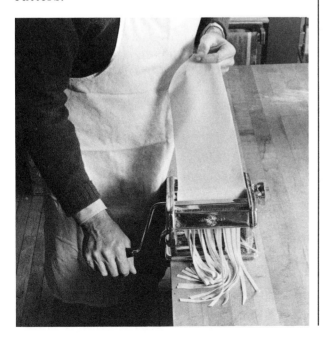

10 You will get perfectly cut fettuccine noodles. Notice how I have reached my hand around and under the machine to grab the noodles as they come out. The noodles are now ready to be dried for later cooking, or they can be cooked at once.

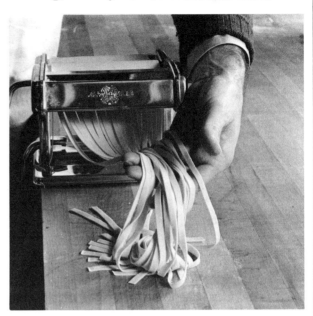

11 By putting the sheet of dough through the narrower cutters you will get a nice tagliarini noodle that goes well with a delicate red sauce or with a clam sauce, among others.

A few extra tips: Do all the rolling and thinning, then do all the cutting. Cover the uncut sheets with a dish towel or paper towels to keep the dough from drying out until you are ready to cut.

12 Once they have been rolled out, the sheets
    of dough can be used to fashion different
    types of pasta, such as lasagna. Cut the
    dough with a jagged-edged cutter to the
    length and width to fit your favorite
    lasagna pan.

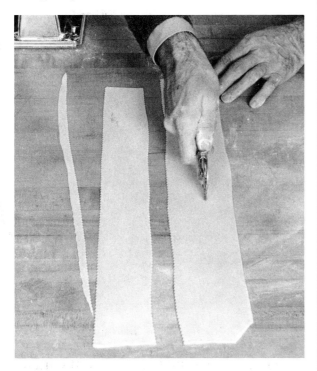

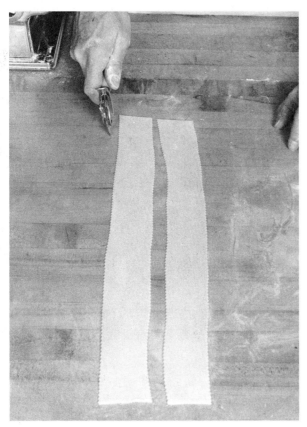

13 Or cut pieces for manicotti or cannelloni.

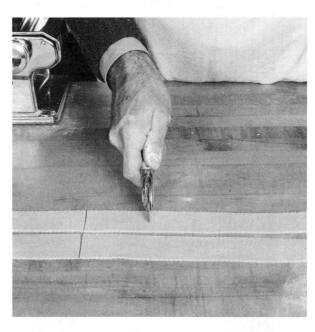

*Other shapes and types of pasta that can be
made from the basic noodle dough will be
covered under the individual recipes.*

Spinach Pasta Dough

1 Cut the dough into 2 pieces. Flatten 1 piece with your hand and start it through the widest setting of the rollers.

2 Dust with flour and fold into thirds as shown in *Basic Pasta Dough*. Put the dough through the rollers again, following the same technique as shown in *Basic Pasta Dough*.

3 Here is an illustration of how to feed the dough through the rollers.

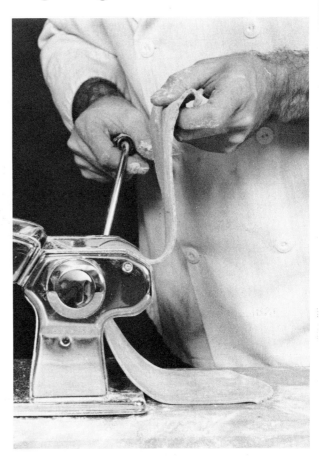

4 After you have kneaded and thinned the dough in the rollers you can cut the dough for fettuccine noodles, as shown. Make sure the dough is not the least bit sticky before cutting or the noodles will not cut properly.

5   The important thing to remember is the constant addition of flour in making spinach pasta. The photo shows dough that is too moist and could not be rolled either by hand or by machine.

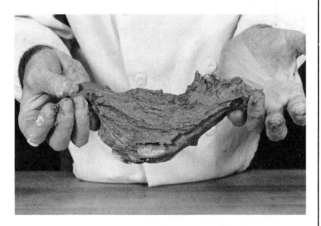

6   Here is an example of dough that was too moist when put through the rollers of the machine. Dust generously with flour, fold into thirds, and put through the widest setting of the rollers again.

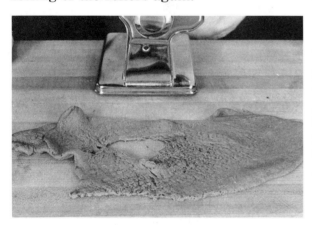

Don't despair if you have problems the first time around. The moisture from the spinach makes the addition of extra flour necessary in this recipe. There is no significant difference in taste in using fresh spinach over frozen. Save yourself a lot of work and use the frozen kind.

6

Rolling and Cutting by Hand

When rolling the dough by hand it is best to let it rest for about 10 minutes beforehand. Cover the ball of dough with a slightly dampened clean dish towel or paper towel to prevent it from drying out.

1   Press down firmly on the dough with the rolling pin, rolling away from your body and then back toward your body.

2   As the dough starts to thin out, do not exert quite as much pressure. If the dough should stick to the rolling pin, dust the dough lightly with flour.

3   As you roll away from your body, angle the rolling pin slightly, first to one side, then to the other. You want to obtain a shape as close to rectangular as possible.

4   Continue rolling, using even lighter
    strokes at this point—almost skimming the
    dough surface. Turn the dough over and
    dust it lightly with flour and continue
    rolling. Avoid putting any holes in the
    dough.

5   If the sheet of dough becomes too large to
    fit onto your work surface, cut it in half to
    make it easier to work with. Try to roll the
    dough quite thin so that you can see your
    hand or the surface of the counter or
    dough board through it.

*If you are working with limited counter
space, it is advisable to cut the ball of dough
into a number of pieces equal to the number
of eggs used prior to the start of the rolling*

*procedure. For example, if you used 2 eggs,
cut the dough into 2 pieces.*

*This sheet of dough can now be used to
make many different types of pasta dishes—
ravioli, lasagna, or tortellini, for examples.
The use of the dough in these recipes and
others will be treated in individual recipes.*

*As an example, the dough can be rolled and
cut into fettuccine noodles as follows:*

6   Before you roll the dough, make certain
    the dough is not the least bit sticky. If it is,
    dust it lightly with flour. Roll the dough
    away from you, keeping the outside edges
    as even as possible.

7   Continue rolling the entire sheet to the
    end.

8   This is a close-up view, from the side, of the completely rolled sheet prior to cutting.

9   Cut the roll into even pieces. The size shown is typical for fettuccine noodles. Tagliarini noodles would be cut half the size of the fettuccine noodles.

10   Unroll the cut pieces as soon as possible to prevent them from sticking together.

11   You now have several choices. The noodles can be cooked immediately, or they can be hung on a pasta drying rack for later cooking, or they can be twirled into nests and allowed to dry for later cooking or storage.

Handling and Storage

Some points concerning handling and storing of pasta dough and noodles: Once the pasta dough has been formed into a ball and fully kneaded, it can be frozen for later use. Dust the ball lightly with flour and put it into a plastic storage bag. Give it ample time to thaw out when you decide to use it. Dough that has been cut into strips will dry out rather fast and will become brittle and break into small pieces. I recommend the following technique.

If cooking the noodles within an hour, use a drying rack or lay out the noodles on a clean dish towel (covering them will slow down the drying). If you wish to store the noodles, it is best to form them into nests (see photo), and store in an airtight canister. Be sure they are completely dry or they will get moldy. To my taste it is best to make the noodles and cook them within an hour.

7

There is no substitute for the fresh, delicate flavor of pasta all'uovo. Pasta all'uovo, as the name implies, is pasta made with flour and eggs and usually handmade. This is contrasted to pasta secche which is made with semolina and water, by machines, in factories, for commercial sale. Pasta all'uovo, which is rolled into sheets either by hand or machine, is the basis for a wide range of pasta types. For example, fettuccine, tagliarini, papparadelle. By varying the thinness, the shape, or the size, you can make tortellini, cappalletti, ravioli, cannelloni, lasagna, and other dishes from the basic dough. Once you have mastered the technique of making pasta all'uovo, the different taste combinations are open to your imagination. That's the good news. The bad news is that you can now buy "freshly made" pasta in a food store, in a department store, in a cookware store, in a trendy delicatessen, and probably, before long, in a hardware store. In a dubious way, this is a tribute to the popularity of the product, but I fear there will be problems in the quality. As in any product, the controls necessary to maintain quality must be enforced—a difficult thing to do when the sales clerk from the luggage department is covering for the "pasta maker" who is on vacation. The very best pasta is that which you make yourself. You, and you alone, maintain the quality; the delicate thinness; the proper texture; the ultimate goodness and fresh taste. Pasta all'uovo is easily made in your own kitchen and offers the pleasure of creating something good to eat—with you the final inspector of quality.

The recipes that follow explore the amazing flexibility of pasta all'uovo. Try one recipe and you will surely go on to try many more.

Tips on Cooking Pasta All'uovo

Freshly made pasta cooks very quickly. If cooked within twenty minutes after cutting, the pasta could be done within one minute.

The longer the pasta has been allowed to dry, the longer it will take to cook—but, without exception, in much less time than dried, packaged pasta.

Test the pasta often for doneness—it may cook quicker than you might expect. If the pasta is extra thin, it will cook even faster.

Always cook the pasta in plenty of boiling salted water, 4 to 5 quarts to the pound.

When you add the pasta, add it in batches to help keep the water at the boiling point.

Basic Procedure for Foolproof Pasta Cooking

1 Bring the water to a vigorous boil.

2 Salt the water. Add 2 tablespoons of salt to 4 quarts of water.

3 Add the pasta to the water and give it a good stir.

4 Test it within 20 to 30 seconds for doneness.

5 Test it every 10 to 15 seconds thereafter, if necessary.

When cooking pasta all'uovo, you must stand over the pot, testing and stirring constantly. A few seconds or minutes of this is little to ask for the enjoyment that follows.

Fettuccine with Butter and Cream

Pasta	1 cup heavy whipping
1½ cups unbleached	cream
flour	⅔ cup freshly grated
2 extra-large eggs	Parmesan cheese
	Salt
Sauce	Freshly ground
3 tablespoons	pepper
unsalted butter	Freshly grated
	nutmeg

Serves 4 as a side dish or a first course

1 Make fettuccine noodles with the flour and eggs, as described in Chapter 2. Then prepare the sauce as follows.

2 Melt the butter in a 9- or 10-inch skillet or sauté pan set over medium heat. Do not let it burn.

3 Add the cream. Turn up the heat to medium high.

4 Bring the butter and cream sauce mixture to a slow boil for about 2 minutes to thicken the sauce slightly. Remove pan from the heat.

5   Bring 4 quarts water to a vigorous boil. Add 1½ tablespoons salt. Drop the noodles into the boiling water a few at a time.

6   Stir thoroughly. Cover the pot. When the water comes back to a boil, remove the cover.

7   As soon as the water comes back to a boil, test for doneness with your teeth. If the pasta was made in the past hour it may be ready at this point. In fact, freshly made pasta cooks within a matter of minutes, so test it often to prevent overcooking. In this dish you will be cooking the pasta a bit more in the sauce, so it is best to undercook it slightly.

8   Return the pan with the butter and cream sauce to the stove over medium heat and quickly add the well-drained pasta to the sauce.

9   Mix the noodles quickly but gently and thoroughly with the butter and cream sauce.

10 Add the Parmesan cheese and incorporate it thoroughly with the noodles and sauce.

11 Add the freshly ground pepper, the salt, and the nutmeg.

12 Serve immediately with additional freshly grated Parmesan.

This dish can easily be done tableside. Bring the cooked noodles and the pan with the butter and cream sauce to the dining room. Have a table burner and the cheese, salt, pepper, and nutmeg ready to use. Serve directly from the pan onto individual serving plates. If you want to reach out for the ultimate taste, shave some white truffles on top of the noodles just before serving.

Fettuccine Primavera

Pasta
2 extra-large eggs
1½ cups unbleached flour

Sauce
6 tablespoons unsalted butter
2 tablespoons flour
1 cup heavy cream
¼ pound Gorgonzola cheese, crumbled
½ pound Fontina cheese, diced

½ cup grated Parmesan cheese
¼ cup chicken broth
Salt
Freshly ground white pepper
2 tablespoons unsalted butter
¼ cup shallots, minced
1 pound zucchini, thinly sliced
1 pound broccoli, blanched
1 cup cooked peas

Serves 4 as a first course or side dish

1 Make fettuccine noodles with the eggs and flour, then mix the sauce, as follows.

2 In a heavy saucepan melt the 6 tablespoons butter over low heat. Add the flour and

30

cook and stir for 2 minutes until the mixture froths. Do not let it brown too much.

3   Add the heavy cream all at once and continue mixing thoroughly while the mixture comes to a boil. Boil for 1 minute, stirring constantly, to thicken the mixture slightly.

4   Add the Gorgonzola, Fontina, and Parmesan cheeses. Turn up the heat slightly and cook and stir until all the cheese is melted.

5   Add the chicken broth and cook and stir for 1 minute. Taste and add salt if necessary. Add the pepper and set aside.

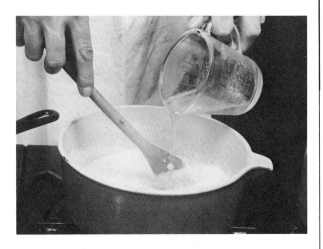

6   In a separate 10- or 12-inch skillet set over medium heat, sauté the shallots in the butter.

7   Add the sliced zucchini to the pan and cook and stir for 3 to 4 minutes until the zucchini is softened slightly. Do not overcook.

8   Cook the broccoli in boiling water 8 to 10 minutes. Add to skillet with the zucchini.

9   Add the sauce to the pan with the vegetables. Turn the heat to medium high and stir and combine the sauce thoroughly with the vegetables. Add the cooked peas and stir again.

10   Put the cooked and drained pasta in a serving dish. Pour the sauce and vegetable mixture over the pasta.

11   Your finished dish. Serve at once.

While the sauce is simmering, prepare the broccoli. Wash it under cold running water. Cut off the stalk close to the head. Peel the thin green skin off the stalks. Divide the head into flowerets. Cut the stalk into bite-sized pieces. Blanch the broccoli in a large pot of boiled salted water—first the stem pieces, about 3 minutes; then the flowerets. Eight minutes should be about the maximum cooking time. When a knife pierces the stalk easily the broccoli is done. Don't overcook the broccoli—it should be on the firm side.
Gorgonzola is a relatively strong cheese. For a milder cheese flavor, substitute Gruyère.

Fettuccine with Italian Sausage

Pasta	2 tablespoons
2 extra-large eggs	unsalted butter
1½ cups unbleached	1 cup heavy cream
flour	½ cup grated
	Parmesan cheese
Sauce	Salt
2 tablespoons olive oil	Pepper
1 pound Italian	
sausage	

Serves 4 as a first course or side dish

1   Make fettuccine noodles using the eggs and flour, then make the sauce, as follows.

2   Slit the sausage casings lengthwise.

3   Peel the casings away from the sausage meat.

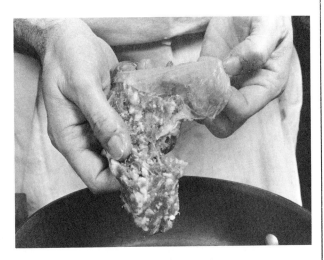

4   Put the oil into a saucepan. Turn the heat to medium high. Crumble the sausage into the pan.

5   Stir and cook the sausage, breaking up any large pieces with a fork or wooden spatula, until cooked through. Remove the sausage from the pan and set aside. Scrape the bottom of the pan with a spatula to release any bits of meat.

6   Reduce heat to medium. Add the butter. When the butter has melted but is not bubbling, add the heavy cream. Cook for 4 to 5 minutes.

7   Add the cooked and drained pasta directly to the butter and cream sauce. Stir gently to coat the noodles. Add the Parmesan cheese. Stir thoroughly. Taste and add salt if necessary.

8   Add the cooked sausage to the noodles. Turn the heat to medium high. Add the pepper. Cook and stir for 2 to 3 minutes.

9   Transfer to a serving dish. Serve at once.

Remember, when the pasta is to have additional cooking in a sauce, it should be slightly undercooked in the water.

Green Fettuccine with Sauce Calabria

Pasta
2   extra-large eggs
2   cups unbleached flour
½   10-ounce package frozen chopped spinach, cooked according to package directions and squeezed dry

Sauce
4   tablespoons olive oil
2   garlic cloves, peeled, sliced lengthwise

1   pound Italian sausage, casings removed
1   can (28 ounces) Italian-style plum tomatoes
2   teaspoons basil
1   teaspoon oregano
1   tablespoon tomato paste
Salt
Pepper

Serves 4 to 5 as a first course or side dish

1   Make green fettuccine using the eggs, flour, and spinach.

2   Heat the oil in a skillet or saucepan. Turn the heat to medium high and sauté the sliced garlic in the oil, pressing lightly on the pieces to release more flavor, until they are lightly browned. Remove the garlic from the pan.

3   Remove the sausage meat from the casings and crumble the sausage into the pan. Break up any large pieces with a fork or wooden spatula. Stir and cook until no traces of red are left in the meat.

4   Turn heat to medium. Add the tomatoes to the pan directly from the can.

5   Mash down on the chunks of tomato with the back of a spoon or a spatula. Add the basil, oregano, and tomato paste. Stir thoroughly. Add salt and pepper to taste. Cook the sauce over low heat for 20 minutes.

6   Put the cooked and drained pasta into a serving dish.

7   Spoon the sauce directly from the pan onto the pasta. Mix thoroughly.

8   Your finished dish. Serve freshly grated Parmesan cheese on the side.

For the sauce, fresh basil is much preferred over dried basil. It fresh basil is available, use 2 or 3 washed leaves broken into little pieces. If fresh Italian plum tomatoes are in season, you will need 7 to 8, blanched, peeled, and chopped. A note on garlic: Sometimes, when the garlic is old, it has a small green vein running through the center of the clove. This should always be removed as it gives the garlic a bitter taste.

Fettuccine with Tomato and Eggplant

Pasta
2 extra-large eggs
1½ cups unbleached
  flour

Sauce
1 medium-sized
  eggplant, peeled
  and diced
½ cup olive oil
1 medium onion,
  finely chopped

2 tablespoons parsley,
  finely chopped
1 can (28 ounces)
  Italian-style plum
  tomatoes
1 teaspoon basil
¼ cup grated
  Parmesan cheese
Salt
Pepper

Serves 4 as a first course or side dish

1   Make fettuccine noodles using eggs and flour, then make the sauce, as follows.

2   Peel and dice the eggplant.

3   In a saute pan, sauté the onion in the oil over medium heat until golden. Remove from pan and set aside.

4   Add the eggplant to the pan. Cook and stir over medium high heat for 3 to 4 minutes. The eggplant may absorb a lot of oil; add more oil if necessary. Return the onions to the pan and add the chopped parsley.

5   Reduce the heat to medium and pour the tomatoes from the can into a food mill.

6 Process the tomatoes directly into the pan.

7 Make sure you scrape the tomato puree from the bottom of the food mill.

8 Add the basil and grated Parmesan to the sauce. Cook the sauce over low heat for 20 minutes.

9 Cook the fettuccine and fork directly onto individual serving plates.

10 Spoon the sauce over the pasta. Serve at once.

11   Serve with additional Parmesan cheese on the side.

Green Fettuccine with Veal

Pasta
2 extra-large eggs
2 cups unbleached flour
½ 10-ounce package frozen chopped spinach, cooked according to package directions and squeezed dry

Sauce
3 tablespoons unsalted butter
2 tablespoons olive oil
Pepper
Flour
½–¾ pound veal scallops, cubed
½ cup dry Marsala
1 cup heavy cream
½ cup grated Parmesan cheese
Salt

Serves 4 as a first course or side dish

1   Make green fettuccine noodles using the eggs, flour, and spinach. Then follow the sauce directions below.

2   Over medium heat, melt the butter with the oil in a 10- or 12-inch skillet or sauté pan, just until the butter starts to foam.

3   Pepper the cubed veal and dredge with flour. Don't flour the veal ahead of time as it will toughen the veal and give it a floury taste.

4   Add the veal to the pan with the butter and oil. Turn up the heat slightly. Sauté the veal until just cooked through. Do not overcook.

5 Remove the veal cubes from the pan and set aside. Add the marsala, turn the heat to high, and cook until no scent of the marsala is left.

6 Turn the heat to medium. Add the heavy cream. Scrape the bottom of the pan to release any bits of veal. Let the cream thicken and reduce slightly. Set aside, if necessary, at this point.

7 Add the cooked and well-drained pasta directly to the pan. Stir to coat all the noodles with the cream.

8 Add the freshly grated Parmesan cheese. Stir gently but thoroughly. Taste and add salt if necessary.

9 Pour the pasta and sauce into a serving dish. Layer the veal over the noodles.

10 Your finished dish—ready to serve.

Florio brand marsala is one of the best. They also make a sweet marsala, but make sure you use the dry marsala for this recipe.

Always choose good-quality veal—the palest pink you can find. For this dish the veal should be pounded, if necessary, to about ¼ inch thick before cubing.

Fresh mushrooms, cleaned, sliced, and sautéed in unsalted butter in a separate skillet, can be added to the sauce just before adding the pasta.

Paglia e Fieno (Yellow and Green Noodles)

This is a very flavorful dish that can be served as an entrée with confidence.

Pasta	*Sauce*
Yellow Pasta:	2 tablespoons shallots, finely chopped
1 extra-large egg	5–6 ounces shredded prosciutto
¾ cup unbleached flour	2 tablespoons unsalted butter
Spinach Pasta:	1 tablespoon olive oil
½ 10-ounce package frozen chopped spinach, cooked according to package directions and squeezed dry	1 cup heavy cream
	1 cup grated Parmesan cheese
	Salt
	Pepper
1 extra-large egg	Nutmeg, freshly grated
1 cup unbleached flour	1 cup cooked peas

Serves 4 as a first course or side dish

1   Make yellow fettuccine with 1 egg and ¾ cup flour. Then make green fettuccine using spinach, 1 egg, and 1 cup flour. Make sauce according to directions .

2   Sauté the shallots and the shredded prosciutto in the butter and oil over medium heat for 2 to 3 minutes. Use a sauté pan about 10 inches in diameter.

3   Add the cream to the pan and stir lightly.

4   Bring the cream to a slow boil to thicken it slightly. Take the pan off heat and set aside.

5 Add the green and yellow noodles to 4 to 5 quarts of boiling salted water. Stir thoroughly and cover pot until water returns to a boil. Remove cover.

6 Test the noodles often for doneness. Remember that they will be cooking some more in the sauce. Drain thoroughly and quickly. Add all at once to the sauce.

7 Turn the heat to medium and stir gently but thoroughly to coat the noodles with the cream mixture.

8 Add the Parmesan cheese. Stir and toss with 2 forks. Taste and add salt if necessary. Add the ground pepper (use white pepper if you have it) and the grated nutmeg.

9 Add the cooked and drained peas directly to the pan. Watch the heat; make sure it is not too high. Mix thoroughly so that the sauce coats all the pasta.

10 Now spoon directly out of the pan into a preheated serving dish or onto individual serving plates.

11 Your finished dish. Serve at once.

It is always wise to have extra freshly grated Parmesan cheese to serve on the side for real cheese lovers. Although the spinach pasta cooks slightly faster than the yellow pasta, it is not necessary to cook them in separate pots.

Green Tagliarini with Scallops

Pasta
2 extra-large eggs
1½ cups unbleached flour
½ 10-ounce package frozen chopped spinach, cooked, squeezed dry, and finely chopped

Sauce
1½ tablespoons unsalted butter
1½ tablespoons flour
1 cup clam juice or fish stock
1 cup heavy cream
Salt
1 pound bay scallops *or* 1 pound sea scallops, cut into 2 or 3 pieces each
Freshly ground white pepper

Serves 4 as a first course or side dish

1 Make the pasta using the eggs, flour, and spinach.

Do not make the sauce too thick for this dish. The consistency of the sauce should be that of a light béchamel sauce. Follow the sauce directions.

2 In a heavy saucepan set over medium heat, cook the butter and flour until pale yellow, stirring constantly for about 2 minutes. Add the clam juice.

3 Reduce the heat a little. Cook and stir until the mixture thickens slightly, about 4 to 5 minutes.

4 Add the heavy cream. Bring the mixture to a slow boil, stirring constantly. Cook until the mixture thickens slightly. Remove from the heat. Set aside. Taste and add salt if necessary.

5 Cook the pasta in plenty of boiling salted water. This thin green pasta cooks very quickly. Do not overcook.

6 Drain the pasta and place it on heated serving plates in the shape of a wreath.

7 Return the sauce to the stove over medium heat. Add the scallops.

8 Gently stir the sauce to immerse all the scallops. Cook and stir for 3 to 4 minutes, no longer, to avoid overcooking the scallops. Taste for salt again. Add the pepper to taste.

9 Using a slotted spoon, scoop some of the scallops and the cream from the pan and place in the center well of the pasta.

10 Put some sauce and scallops around the outside edge of the pasta. Serve at once.

This presentation can also be made on a flat oval serving dish. Following the same shape as the plate, arrange the pasta with a well in the center. Put all the scallops and some cream in the center. Ring the outside perimeter of the pasta with the sauce.

Tagliarini with Chicken

Pasta
2 extra-large eggs
1½ cups unbleached flour

Sauce
2 chicken breasts, skinned, boned, and chopped
Pepper
1 tablespoon unsalted butter

2 tablespoons olive oil
1 can (28 ounces) Italian-style plum tomatoes
¾ cup peas
1 tablespoon oregano

2 tablespoons unsalted butter
¼ cup grated Parmesan cheese

Serves 4 as a first course or side dish

1 Make the pasta using the eggs and flour. Then prepare the sauce, as follows.

2 Use boneless chicken breasts or bone your own and save some money. Pat the breasts dry with a paper towel. Chop the breasts. Pepper generously.

3 Put the butter and oil in a sauté pan. Over medium heat, sauté the chicken until it is just cooked through and lightly browned. Scrape the bottom of the pan with a wooden spatula.

4 Put the tomatoes into a food mill and add directly to the pan. Turn up the heat a bit and stir well.

5 Add the peas. If using frozen peas, do not cook or thaw them. Add the oregano. Simmer the sauce for 40 minutes. Stir the sauce occasionally.

6   Cook the pasta in plenty of boiling salted water. Drain well and put into a heated serving bowl. Add the butter and the Parmesan cheese. Mix thoroughly.

7   Spoon the sauce over the pasta. Mix well. Serve at once.

Tagliarini with Chicken Livers

Pasta
2 extra-large eggs
1½ cups unbleached flour

Sauce
1 medium onion, chopped
2 tablespoons unsalted butter
½ pound ground chuck
1 can (28 ounces) Italian-style plum tomatoes

1 tablespoon parsley, finely chopped
½ pound chicken livers
2 tablespoons unsalted butter
½ cup dry marsala
Salt
Pepper

½ cup Parmesan cheese

Serves 4 as a first course or side dish

1   Make the tagliarini with the eggs and flour. Follow the directions given below for the sauce.

2   In a sauté pan set over medium heat, sauté the onion in the butter until the onions are a pale yellow. Add the ground chuck, breaking it up with your fingers, and cook until no traces of red are left. Stir well and scrape the bottom of the pan with a wooden spatula. Break up any large chunks of meat with the spatula.

45

3   Pass the tomatoes through a food mill into the pan with the ground chuck. Stir well. Bring the sauce to a slow boil. Turn down the heat to maintain a slow simmer. Add the chopped parsley.

4   In a separate skillet, sauté the chicken livers in the butter over medium heat until they are just cooked through.

5   Turn up the heat and add the dry marsala. Cook and stir until the wine has cooked away.

6   Add the cooked livers to the pan with the tomatoes and meat. Taste and add salt if necessary. Add pepper to taste. Simmer the sauce over low heat for 30 minutes.

7   Cook the pasta in plenty of boiling salted water. Notice this method of adding the pasta to the boiling water.

8   Drain the pasta or scoop it out of the pot into a heated serving bowl.

9   Add the sauce to the bowl with the pasta
     and stir well to incorporate the sauce. Add
     the grated Parmesan. Stir again. Serve at
     once.

Tagliarini with Prosciutto

This is a very simple, tasty recipe that makes
an excellent last-minute pasta dish. If you are
out of prosciutto, substitute boiled ham.

Pasta
2 extra-large eggs
1½ cups unbleached
   flour

Sauce
½ cup chopped onion
2 tablespoons
   unsalted butter
¼ pound prosciutto,
   thinly sliced

½ cup water
¾ cup peas (fresh or
   frozen)
3 tablespoons
   unsalted butter
½ cup grated
   Parmesan cheese
Salt
Pepper

Serves 4 as a first course or side dish

1   Make the pasta using the eggs and flour.
     Then follow the sauce directions.

2   In a sauté pan set over medium heat, sauté
     the onion in the butter for 2 to 3 minutes.
     Don't let the onions get too soft. Add the
     sliced prosciutto and cook for 3 to 4
     minutes or until the prosciutto is lightly
     cooked but not browned. (Don't burn the
     onions.)

3   Add the water to the pan. Add the peas
     and stir well until the peas are cooked.
     Turn the heat to low until the pasta is
     ready. Add more water if the sauce gets
     too dry. For this dish you can use frozen
     peas right out of the box.

4   Cook the pasta in plenty of boiling salted
     water. Drain the pasta and put into a
     heated serving bowl. Add the butter and
     the Parmesan and stir well to incorporate.

5 Add the peas and prosciutto to the bowl with the pasta and stir well. Taste and add salt if necessary. Add pepper to taste.

Pasta Mezzaluna

Pasta
Spinach Pasta:
1 extra-large egg
1 cup unbleached flour
1 egg-sized lump cooked chopped spinach

Yellow Pasta:
1 extra-large egg
¾ cup unbleached flour

Sauces
Tomato Sauce (see *Cavatelli with Tomato Sauce*, page 76)
Béchamel Sauce (see page 61)

Filling
2 pounds chicken, skinned, cooked, chopped
2 whole eggs
½ cup grated Parmesan cheese
¼ cup parsley, finely chopped
Salt
Pepper

3 ounces prosciutto, sliced paper thin
½ cup freshly grated Parmesan cheese

Order of Preparation
Make the spinach pasta and the yellow pasta.
Make the filling and refrigerate.
Make the tomato sauce.
Make the béchamel sauce.

Makes 6 serving portions—3 to a serving

This dish sounds complicated but it really isn't. Much of the work can be done ahead. Roll out the pasta and cook the triangles right away. Once cooked, they can rest for about 2 hours. The filling and the sauces can be made well ahead of time, but don't let the béchamel sauce get too thick.

1 Make the green and yellow pastas and roll each into a long rectangular shape by hand or using a pasta machine.

2 Cut the pasta into triangular shapes. Cut one and use this piece as a guide to cut the others.

3   Reverse the model piece as you go to make all the pieces approximately the same size.

4   As you can see, the two pieces of pasta yielded 18 pasta triangles, ready for cooking. Actually, you may have a bit of the spinach pasta left over. Freeze it for later use.

5   Cook the pasta triangles, a few at a time, in plenty of boiling salted water. Try to keep the water at the boiling point. Cook for less than 2 minutes.

6   Scoop out the pasta as it is cooked and put into a large bowl of cold water. Lay out the pieces on a clean, slightly dampened dish towel. Pat the tops dry with a paper towel. Let the pasta sit for 45 minutes to an hour. Now make the filling.

7   Put the chicken pieces into a pot of cold water and poach over high heat until cooked through. Drain and cool. Pull the meat off the bones and chop very finely. Add the eggs and mix well. Add the Parmesan cheese and the parsley.

8   Mix the filling ingredients thoroughly. You should have a pasty consistency. Taste and add salt if necessary. Add pepper to taste.

To make the filling in the food processor: Put the skinned and cooked chicken, eggs, Parmesan, and parsley into the work bowl fitted with the steel blade. Pulse in 10-second bursts 3 or 4 times until all the ingredients are combined. If the mixture seems too dry, add a bit of chicken broth or water.

Refrigerate the filling. Next, make the tomato sauce.

9   While the sauce is cooking, fill and roll the pasta.

Lay a thin slice of prosciutto on top of the pasta triangle.

10 Form the filling into small sausagelike rolls and lay one roll on top of each slice of prosciutto.

11 Roll the pasta away from you to enclose the filling.

12 Continue in this fashion until all the triangles have been filled and rolled. This is how they will look. Next, make the béchamel sauce.

13 Liberally butter an ovenproof serving dish. Spread a thin layer of tomato sauce in the bottom of the dish.

14 Lay the pasta triangles in the dish. Use two smaller dishes if your largest one will not hold all the triangles.

15 Spoon the béchamel sauce between the pasta triangles. Sprinkle some grated Parmesan over the pasta.

16 Spoon some of the tomato sauce around the edge of the dish. Spoon the remainder of the béchamel sauce into the center. Reserve some of the tomato sauce.

17 Sprinkle some Parmesan over the béchamel sauce in the center.

18 Here is the dish ready for baking. Bake in a preheated 400° F. oven for 40 to 50 minutes, or until the sauce bubbles and the center is lightly browned. Serve immediately, directly from the baking dish with extra sauce on the side.

An alternate presentation: Use a spatula and lift out of the baking dish onto individual plates, three pieces for each serving. Lay them on the plate like spokes in a wheel. Put some of the extra sauce between the pasta rolls. Serve at once.

Pasta Roll

Pasta
1 extra-large egg
1 egg yolk
1½ cups unbleached
  flour
1–2 tablespoons warm
  water

Filling

1 10-ounce package
  frozen chopped
  spinach, cooked
  according to
  package directions
  and squeezed dry

2 tablespoons
  unsalted butter
2 cups ricotta
2 eggs
½ cup grated
  Parmesan cheese
Salt
Freshly ground
  pepper
Freshly grated
  nutmeg

¼ pound unsalted
  butter
½ cup grated
  Parmesan cheese

Serves 4 as a first course or side dish

1   Make the pasta and roll into a rectangular shape about 14 inches by 10 inches and not quite paper thin. Set aside while you make the filling. Cover the pasta with a clean, dampened dishcloth to keep it from drying.

2   After you have cooked the spinach and squeezed it dry, sauté it in the 2 tablespoons of butter for 2 to 3 minutes over medium heat, stirring to coat the spinach with the butter. Cool slightly and chop finely.

3   Make the filling by combining the ricotta, spinach, eggs, ½ cup grated Parmesan, salt and pepper to taste, and three strokes of whole nutmeg against a nutmeg grater.

4   Stir the mixture vigorously to blend completely.

5   Now spread the filling evenly over the sheet of pasta.

6   Leave a ¾-inch border on all four sides of the sheet of pasta.

7   Carefully and gently roll it up, starting from the end closest to you.

8   When you get near the end, pick up the pasta end still showing and bring it up on top of the roll.

9   Cut a piece of good-quality cheesecloth large enough to enclose the pasta roll with two thicknesses of the cloth. The cheesecloth should be fairly tight so that the pasta roll does not lose its shape during poaching.

10   Now tie the two ends snugly and tightly. Cut off any excess cheesecloth from the two ends.

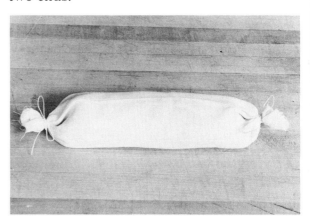

11 Gently lower the pasta roll into a large pot of boiling water. The pot should be large enough and deep enough to enable the roll to float freely. (An oval roaster works very well.) Poach the roll in the boiling water for 20 minutes.

12 Carefully remove the roll from the water with a large slotted skimmer or 2 large wooden spatulas. Let the roll sit in the cheesecloth for about 5 minutes to firm up. Cut the tied "ears" off each end of the roll and remove the cheesecloth. Let the roll sit for another 5 minutes and transfer it to an oval ovenproof serving dish.

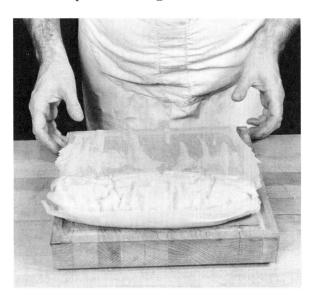

13 Cut the roll into 1-inch slices. Cut the ¼ pound of butter into 8 pieces and lay it along the center of the roll. Sprinkle on the ½ cup grated Parmesan. Place in a preheated 400° F. oven for 15 minutes until the butter melts and the cheese is lightly browned.

14 Your finished dish, ready for serving.

For a more robust flavor, serve with a red sauce (see Cavatelli with Tomato Sauce, *page 76). You can get 10 slices, 1-inch thick, from this recipe. Two slices per serving is ample as a first course.*

1 The proper size sheet of dough for this recipe can be made using the pasta machine by seaming two sheets of dough together.

2 Use ¾ of the ball of dough and roll out 2 sheets of pasta in the machine as described earlier.

3 Stop at the next-to-last setting for the correct thickness.

4 Wet the long edge of 1 strip of dough. Place the other strip on top with an overlap of about ½ inch.

5 Roll over the seam with a rolling pin on both sides to seal the strips together. The dough is now ready for the filling.

Basic Lasagna

Lasagna, simply stated, is layers of pasta with a filling and a sauce in between. Anybody who has eaten lasagna—and it would be hard to find someone who has not—knows that it can be a most satisfying and delicious dish to serve.

There are as many lasagna recipes as there are cooks in Italy. Lasagna—as well as tortellini and cannelloni—gives an opportunity to use that leftover cooked chicken or turkey, ground beef, ham, chicken livers, and vegetables. This is usually how a "new" lasagna dish is created in an Italian home; and it becomes a sensible and frugal approach to a most enjoyable meal.

In my opinion, there is a vast difference between lasagna made with homemade pasta and that made with packaged pasta. The lightness and delicate taste of the homemade pasta is what makes a lasagna dish something more than layers of pasta with a filling and a sauce.

Some basic rules to follow:

The pasta strips or squares for lasagna should be fairly thin. If you use the pasta machine, the next to last setting of the rollers is the ideal thinness for the pasta. If rolling by hand, you should see the outline of your hand through the dough.

If using the pasta machine: A recipe that calls for 2 extra-large eggs and 1½ cups of flour will yield 8 strips of pasta that will fit into a rectangular baking pan that measures 13 to 14 inches long by 7 to 7½ inches wide, considering that the pasta strips will increase in size during cooking.

If rolling by hand: Use 3 extra-large eggs and 2¼ cups of flour, since pasta made by hand is never quite as thin as that made with the machine.

The depth of the baking dish for lasagna, using 4 layers of pasta, should be a minimum of 2 inches.

The baking of the finished assembled lasagna will continue to cook the pasta. Therefore, the pasta must be undercooked—2 to 3 minutes in the boiling water if the pasta is freshly made.

After the pasta has been cooked it should be transferred to a bowl of cold water and then laid out on clean towels that have been rinsed and squeezed dry of excess water.

The assembled lasagna takes nicely to freezing. Those one or two leftover portions can be wrapped in plastic and foil after they have cooled, put into the freezer, and rebaked another time.

The assembled lasagna can be made ahead (up to 1 day), refrigerated, and baked prior to serving time.

Reserve some of the sauce used in making the lasagna for passing at the table.

Preparing Pasta for Lasagna

1   Prepare pasta dough for cutting.

2   The dough that I am cutting is the width that you would get from an Atlas or Imperia pasta machine with 5½-inch-wide rollers. Cutting the dough down the center will give you 2 lasagna strips that will fit into a 7-inch-wide rectangular baking dish, after the pasta has been cooked.

3   This is how your cut strips of dough should look.

4   Size the length of the strips to fit the dish in which you will bake the lasagna. Cut them about 2 inches shorter than the length of the dish since the pasta will swell in size during cooking.

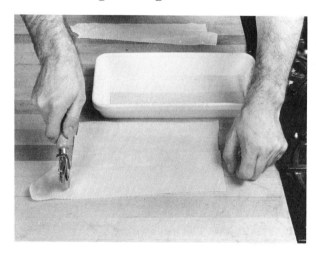

5   Cook the lasagna strips a few at a time in plenty of boiling salted water.

6   When they are cooked, drain them into a large bowl of cold water.

7   While the next batch of pasta is cooking, separate the strips of cooked pasta.

8   Lay them out on slightly damp towels and gently pat them dry. Let the pasta rest for about 10 minutes. The pasta is now ready for the lasagna assembly.

Lasagna with Italian Sausage

Pasta
2 extra-large eggs
1½ cups unbleached
   flour

Sauce
2 cloves garlic, sliced
2 tablespoons olive oil
1 pound Italian
   sausage
1 can (28 ounces)
   Italian-style plum
   tomatoes
1 teaspoon fennel
1 teaspoon basil
1 teaspoon oregano
Salt to taste

Cheese Filling
3 cups ricotta cheese
2 eggs
2 tablespoons chopped
   parsley
⅓ cup grated
   Parmesan cheese
Salt to taste
Freshly ground
   pepper

1 cup or more grated
   mozzarella cheese

Order of Preparation:
Make the pasta strips.
Make the sauce.
Cook the pasta.
Make the cheese
   filling.
Assemble the lasagna.

Makes 6 to 8 portions as a main course

1   Make the pasta strips using the 2 extra-large eggs and 1½ cups flour.

2   To make the sauce: Over medium heat, sauté the garlic (sliced vertically) in the oil until light brown; do not burn. Discard the garlic. Remove the sausage from the casings, add it to the pan, and stir and cook, scraping the bottom of the pan to free any bits of sausage that may stick, until the sausage is fully cooked. Process the tomatoes through a food mill directly into the pan. Add the seasonings. Taste and add salt if necessary. Once the sauce has come to a boil, reduce the heat to low to maintain a steady simmer (an occasional small bubble). Simmer the sauce for 1 hour. Stir thoroughly every so often. If the sauce reduces and thickens too much, add about ½ cup of beef broth.

3   To cook the pasta: Cook, drain, and dry the pasta strips as shown in the introduction to this section.

4   To make the cheese filling: Combine all the ingredients (not including the mozzarella)

as listed. Beat the mixture completely and thoroughly with a wooden spoon. Refrigerate until the lasagna is to be assembled.

5   Preheat the oven to 400° F. Liberally butter the sides and bottom of an ovenproof baking dish.

6   Spread a thin layer of sauce in the bottom of the pan.

7   Place a layer of pasta on top of the sauce.

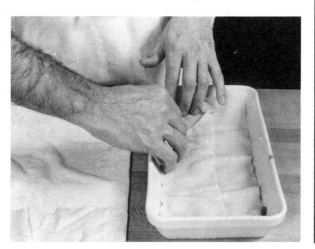

8   Spread some of the ricotta mixture on top of the pasta.

9   Add another layer of pasta.

10   Then put another layer of sauce on top of the pasta.

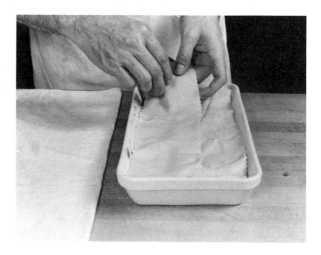

11   Add another layer of pasta.

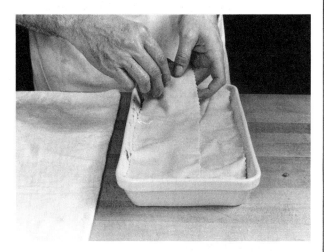

12   Spread on another layer of ricotta.

13   Add the last layer of pasta.

14   Top the last layer of pasta with sauce. Finish by grating the mozzarella directly on top.

15   Here is the dish ready for baking. Bake in a preheated 400° F. oven for 30 to 35 minutes until the sauce starts to bubble and the cheese has melted.

Allow to cool for 10 to 15 minutes before cutting.

Lasagna with Chicken

Pasta
2 extra-large eggs
1½ cups unbleached
 flour

Sauce
½ cup chopped onions
½ cup chopped carrots
2 tablespoons
 unsalted butter
2 tablespoons olive oil
1 can (28 ounces)
 Italian-style plum
 tomatoes
2 tablespoons finely
 chopped parsley
Salt to taste

Filling
2 cups chicken,
 cooked and skinned
3 ounces prosciutto
2 eggs
¼ cup grated
 Parmesan cheese
Chicken broth
Salt to taste
Freshly ground
 pepper

½ cup or more grated
 Parmesan cheese

Order of Preparation:
Make the pasta strips.
Make the sauce.
Cook the pasta.
Make the chicken
 filling.
Process the sauce.
Assemble the lasagna.

Makes 6 to 8 portions as a main course

1   To make the pasta strips: Roll out the pasta and cut it into 8 strips as explained in the introduction to this section.

2   To make the sauce: In a heavy (not aluminum) pan, sauté the onions and the carrots in the butter and oil over medium heat until slightly softened. Add the tomatoes and their juice to the pan. Add the chopped parsley. Once the sauce has come to a boil, reduce the heat to low to maintain a steady simmer (an occasional small bubble). Simmer the sauce for 45 minutes.

3   To cook the pasta: Cook, drain, and dry the pasta as shown in the introduction to this section.

4   To make the chicken filling: Put the cooked chicken in a food processor (with the steel blade) or in a blender, until finely chopped. Chop the prosciutto, add to the chicken, and process or blend a few seconds more. Put this mixture into a bowl. Add the eggs and the ¼ cup grated

Parmesan. Mix thoroughly with a wooden spoon. The mixture should be somewhat liquid and spreadable. If it isn't, add enough chicken broth to achieve that consistency. Taste and add salt if necessary. Add the freshly ground pepper. Refrigerate until the lasagna is to be assembled.

5   Just before assembling the lasagna, process the sauce through a food mill. Place the food mill on top of a bowl and spoon the sauce into the mill.

6   Process the sauce through the mill into the bowl.

7   This should be the consistency of the tomato sauce. If not, add some chicken broth and stir thoroughly.

8   Assemble the lasagna as follows:
Liberally butter the baking dish, sides and bottom.
Lay down a thin layer of sauce.
Lay down 2 strips of pasta.
Lay down a layer of chicken filling.
Lay down 2 strips of pasta.
Lay down a layer of sauce.
Lay down 2 strips of pasta.
Lay down a layer of chicken filling.
Lay down 2 strips of pasta.
Top off with the sauce.
Sprinkle the top generously with ½ cup or more grated Parmesan cheese.

9   Bake in a preheated 375° F. oven for 35 to 40 minutes until the sauce starts to bubble. Allow to cool for 10 to 15 minutes before cutting and serving.

Lasagna with Bolognese and Béchamel Sauces

Pasta
2 extra-large eggs
2 cups unbleached flour
½ 10-ounce package frozen chopped spinach, cooked, squeezed dry, and finely chopped
Extra flour as needed

Bolognese Sauce
¼ cup chopped onions
¼ cup chopped carrots
¼ cup chopped celery
3 tablespoons unsalted butter
3 tablespoons olive oil
1 pound ground chuck
½ cup dry white wine
½ cup milk

1 can (28 ounces) Italian-style plum tomatoes
Salt
½ cup heavy cream

Béchamel Sauce
6 tablespoons unsalted butter
6 tablespoons unbleached flour
2 cups milk
Salt

Order of Preparation:
Make the bolognese sauce.
Make and cook the pasta.
Make the béchamel sauce.
Assemble the lasagna.

Makes 6 to 8 portions as a main course

1   For making the bolognese sauce, chop the onions, celery, and carrots.

2   In a deep, heavy (4½- to 5-quart) pan, sauté the vegetables in the butter and oil over medium heat until they are slightly softened.

3   Add the ground chuck, crumbling it with your fingers.

4   Stir the mixture, breaking up the meat with a spoon.

5   Sauté the mixture until the meat loses its red color.

6   Turn the heat to high. Add the wine. Cook and stir until the wine is cooked off.

7   Add the milk. Cook and stir until the milk has evaporated.

8   Coarsely chop the tomatoes in their juice.

9   Add the tomatoes to the pan with the meat and vegetables. Stir thoroughly. When the sauce starts to bubble, turn the heat down. Keep the sauce at a slow simmer for a minimum of 2 hours. Just before using the sauce in the lasagna, stir in the heavy cream.

10   About 45 minutes before the sauce is done, make the pasta. Roll it out and cut the pasta strips as described in the introduction to this section. Cook the pasta. Lay out the cooked pasta on damp towels.

11   Make the béchamel sauce following the directions for *Lasagna Mescolato* (page 64).

12   Assemble the lasagna as follows:
Liberally butter the baking dish, bottom and sides.
Lay down a thin layer of bolognese sauce.
Lay down 2 strips of pasta.
Lay down a layer of béchamel sauce.
Lay down 2 strips of pasta.
Lay down a layer of bolognese sauce.
Lay down 2 strips of pasta.
Lay down a layer of béchamel sauce.
Lay down 2 strips of pasta.
Top off with bolognese sauce.

13   Bake in the middle of a preheated 375° F. oven for 45 minutes, until the sauce starts to bubble. Allow to cool for 10 to 15 minutes before serving. It is a good idea to place the baking dish on a piece of aluminum foil to catch any sauce that may boil over during baking.

Lasagna with Beef and Veal

Pasta
2 extra-large eggs
1½ cups unbleached
   flour

Sauce
1½ ounces dried
   mushrooms
2 tablespoons
   unsalted butter
½ cup finely chopped
   onions
½ pound ground
   chuck
½ pound ground veal
1 can (28 ounces)
   Italian-style plum
   tomatoes
2 tablespoons tomato
   paste
About ½ cup beef
   broth
Salt to taste

Cheese Filling
2½ cups ricotta cheese
1 10-ounce package
   frozen chopped
   spinach, cooked,
   squeezed dry, and
   finely chopped
2 eggs
¼ cup grated
   Parmesan cheese
Salt to taste

1 cup or more grated
   mozzarella cheese

Order of Preparation:
Make the pasta.
Make the sauce.
Cook the pasta.
Make the cheese
   filling.
Assemble the lasagna.

Makes 6 to 8 portions as a main course

1   Make the pasta using the extra-large eggs and the flour.

2 To make the sauce: Soak the dried mushrooms in warm water for 15 minutes, drain, rinse thoroughly in cold water to remove any sand, and chop finely.

Over medium heat, melt the butter in a heavy (nonaluminum) sauté pan or casserole. Add the chopped onions. Cook and stir until the onions are transparent. Add the ground chuck and veal. Stir and cook—break up lumps of meat with a wooden spatula—until no traces of red are left in the meats. Add the finely chopped mushrooms. Pass the tomatoes through a food mill directly into the pan with the meats. Stir thoroughly. Add the tomato paste. Stir again.

Once the sauce has come to a boil, reduce the heat to low to maintain a steady simmer (an occasional bubble). Simmer the sauce for 1½ hours. Taste and add salt if necessary. Stir the sauce thoroughly every so often. If the sauce reduces and thickens too much, add some beef broth. (See *Lasagna with Chicken* recipe for proper consistency.)

3 To cook the pasta: Cook, drain, and dry the pasta strips as shown in the introduction to this section.

4 To make the cheese filling: In a large bowl, combine the ricotta, spinach, eggs, and Parmesan. Beat thoroughly and vigorously with a wooden spoon. Taste and add salt if necessary. Refrigerate until ready to use.

5 Assemble the lasagna as follows:
Liberally butter the sides and bottom of the baking dish.
Lay down a thin layer of sauce.
Lay down 2 strips of pasta.
Lay down a layer of cheese filling.
Lay down 2 strips of pasta.
Lay down a layer of sauce.
Lay down 2 strips of pasta.
Lay down a layer of cheese filling.
Lay down 2 strips of pasta.
Top with sauce.
Top the sauce with 1 cup or more grated mozzarella.

6 Bake in a preheated 400° F. oven for 35 to 40 minutes, until the sauce starts to bubble and the mozzarella melts. Allow to cool for 10 to 15 minutes before cutting and serving.

Lasagna Mescolato

This recipe is an adaptation of one created by Luciano Parolari, executive chef at Villa d'Este, Lake Como, Italy, where some of the best food in Italy is served.

Pasta
2 extra-large eggs
2 cups unbleached flour
½ 10-ounce package frozen chopped spinach, cooked, squeezed dry, and finely chopped
Extra flour as needed

Meat Sauce
2 tablespoons unsalted butter
2 tablespoons olive oil
1 cup chopped onions
1 cup chopped carrots
1 cup chopped celery
½ pound ground chuck
½ pound Italian sausage, casing removed
1 cup dry red wine
1 can (28 ounces) Italian-style plum tomatoes
2 tablespoons tomato paste

½ cup dried mushrooms (porcini)
2 tablespoons chopped parsley
Salt and freshly ground pepper

Béchamel Sauce
3 tablespoons unsalted butter
3 tablespoons unbleached flour
2 cups milk
¼ teaspoon freshly ground nutmeg
Salt

½ cup freshly grated Parmesan cheese

Order of Preparation:
Make the meat sauce.
Make and cook the pasta.
Make the béchamel sauce.
Mix the lasagna.

Serves 6 to 8 as a main course

The sauce can be made a day ahead, up to the point of adding the seasoning, and refrigerated. If the sauce should reduce and thicken too much, add some beef broth or hot water. The sauce should simmer for a minimum of 45 minutes but no longer than 1 hour.

1 Make the meat sauce as follows: In a 4- to 5-quart heavy (nonaluminum) pan set over medium heat, melt the butter with the oil. Add the chopped vegetables. Cook and stir until the vegetables are slightly softened. Set aside.

2 In a separate 10- to 12-inch sauté pan or skillet, sauté the ground chuck and the sausage over medium heat until no traces of red are left in the meats. Turn the heat to high. Add the wine. Cook and stir until any scent of the wine has gone. Take the pan off the heat.

3 Drain off the excess fat from the pan. Pass the tomatoes through a food mill into the pan with the meats. Add the tomato paste. Cook the sauce over medium heat for 10 minutes, stirring occasionally.

4 While the sauce is cooking, soak the dried mushrooms in warm water until softened. Rinse thoroughly, drain off the water, and chop finely. Add to the pan with the tomatoes.

5 Pour the tomato and meat sauce into the pan with the softened vegetables. Add the chopped parsley. Add salt and pepper to taste. Let the sauce simmer slowly over low heat, stirring occasionally, while you make the pasta.

6   The pasta should be rolled fairly thin (next-to-last setting on the pasta machine).

7   Cut the pasta into rectangular shapes approximately 2 inches by 3 inches. Use all the pasta, including the scraps.

8   Have a large bowl filled with cold water ready to receive the cooked pasta. Cook the pasta in plenty of boiling salted water, a few pieces at a time. Keep the water at a full boil.

9   Cook the freshly made pasta for 2 to 3 minutes. It should be slightly undercooked. Retrieve the cooked pasta from the boiling water with a strainer or perforated skimmer and transfer it to the bowl of cold water. Continue until all the pasta is cooked. Green pasta cooks faster than yellow pasta. Test the pasta as you are cooking. Use your hands to separate any pieces of the cooked pasta that might stick together in the cold water. Leave the pasta in the cold water while you make the béchamel sauce.

10 To make the béchamel: Use a heavy 2½- to
3-quart saucepan. Melt the butter over
medium heat until it just starts to froth.
Add the flour and stir constantly with a
wooden spoon. Cook and stir until the color
is golden brown. Make sure to get all the
flour from the bottom and sides of the pan.
Total cooking time should be 2 to 3
minutes. Don't let it get too dark in color.
Remove from the heat and set aside.

11 In another saucepan heat the milk until it
is just short of boiling.

12 Put the saucepan with the cooked butter
and flour back on low heat and at once add
the hot milk in a constant, steady stream,
stirring constantly. Turn the heat up
slightly. Keep stirring until the sauce
reaches a boil. Cook and stir for about 5 to
6 minutes, keeping the sauce at a slow
bubbly boil. Remove from the heat. Add
the grated nutmeg and stir again. Add salt
to taste.

13 Drain the water from the bowl holding the
pasta. Pour about ¾ of the bechamel over
the pasta. (Notice the not-too-thick
consistency of the béchamel.)

14 Spoon about half the meat sauce on top of
the béchamel. Stir the contents of the bowl
completely and thoroughly. Add the grated
Parmesan.

15   Add the rest of the meat sauce and stir again.

16   Pour the mixture into an oval or rectangular baking dish. You will need one that is approximately 8 inches by 10 inches.

17   Spoon the remaining béchamel on top. Bake in a preheated 375° F. oven for 30 to 35 minutes until it starts to bubble and the béchamel on top starts to brown slightly.

18   Your finished dish. Serve at once.

Basic Ravioli

Like lasagna, ravioli has become a well-known word in the English language. Webster's *New World Dictionary* defines ravioli as small casings of dough, often square, containing seasoned ground meat, cheese, etc., boiled and usually served in a savory sauce. Some purists might disagree a bit with that definition in that only cases filled with ricotta cheese are properly called ravioli. With any other stuffing they are called agnolotti. Stating that, I have made my peace with the purists. For the purposes of this book we shall call them ravioli, regardless of the stuffing.

   Here are three different methods for making ravioli.

   Method One

1   Roll out a sheet of dough using the basic pasta dough recipe. This size sheet of dough was obviously done with a rolling pin, not a pasta machine. Do not allow the dough to dry too long; this will prevent the ravioli from sealing properly. Brush ½ the dough with an egg wash (a beaten egg and a bit of cold water).

2 Put a quantity of filling in a pastry bag fitted with an open pastry tube (No. 5 or 6).

3 Pipe the filling, making small, equally spaced mounds, onto the side of the dough with the egg wash. If you don't care to use a pastry bag, drop the filling off the end of a spoon.

4 Lift the other ½ of the sheet and fold it over the mounds of filling, keeping the edges as even as possible.

5 Using the tips of your fingers, press down firmly around the mounds of filling. Work from the closed side (my left hand) toward the open side to squeeze out any air pockets.

6 Using a cutter-sealer—this one is called the Krimp-Kut Sealer—cut between the rows of filling in both directions and along the four edges to shape and cut the ravioli.

Method Two

1 In this method we will use a pasta machine to roll out the dough and a ravioli form to cut and seal the ravioli. Roll out a sheet of dough (stopping at the next-to-last setting on the rollers). Roll 1 long sheet as shown, or 2 single sheets.

2 Size the sheet so that it is slightly longer and wider than the ravioli form. You can facilitate this by putting the form on top of the dough and cutting two sheets to the proper size.

3 Be sure that the bottom of the sheet—the side laying against the mold—is well floured to prevent the dough from sticking to the mold. Lay the sheet on the mold.

4 Press gently down into the holes with the top part of the ravioli form. This forms the pockets that will hold the filling. Notice the trailing edge of dough that you will want on all four sides of the mold.

5 Remove the top part of the mold and put the filling into the pockets. Here I am dropping the filling off the end of a spoon. You can, of course, use a pastry bag to do this as shown in Method One. Do not use an excessive amount of filling or the ravioli may split during boiling.

6 Place another sheet of dough on top of the filling.

7   Press down gently on top of the pockets of
    filling so that the top of the mold is flat.

8   Roll a pin over the form—lengthwise and
    across the width—until the jagged cutting
    edges of the form are visible through the
    dough. You will see the defined square
    shape of the 12 ravioli. Pull away the
    scraps of dough from around the edges of
    the mold. These can be rerolled into sheets
    to make more ravioli.

9   Tilt the form directly onto a cookie sheet
    or jelly roll pan and the ravioli will fall out
    of the form. If any stick to the form, push
    them out gently, through the holes, with
    your thumb.

Method Three

1   In this method we will use a sheet of
    dough rolled through a pasta machine, but
    not the ravioli form. Again, use 1 long
    sheet of dough or 2 single sheets. Here I
    am folding 1 long sheet in half.

2   Square off the end of the sheet of dough.

3   Brush ½ the dough with an egg wash.

4   Pipe even rows of filling on the side of the dough with the egg wash.

5   Fold the other ½ of the dough over the filling.

6   Using your fingertips, press down between the mounds of filling lengthwise and widthwise, working from the center toward the open edges to force out the air.

7   Cut between the mounds of filling with a jagged cutter or a Krimp-Cut Sealer to cut and seal the ravioli.

Cooking and Storing Ravioli

1   If the ravioli are to be cooked at once, drop them off the jelly roll pan, a few at a time, into plenty of boiling salted water. If the ravioli are cooked directly after making them, they will cook in about 4 to 5 minutes. You can test by scooping one onto a plate and cutting off a small edge of dough with a fork. If they are done, it will cut easily.

2 When they are done, scoop them out of the water quickly with a slotted spoon or strainer into a serving dish or bowl. Dress them with the sauce and serve at once.

Additional Tips

If the ricotta cheese has an excessive amount of water, squeeze it in cheesecloth or allow it to sit in a strainer over a pan for 10 to 15 minutes.

You can make the ravioli ahead of time, up to 2 to 3 hours, and store it in the refrigerator.

If you are having trouble with your dough being too stiff, add a tablespoon of olive oil to your basic flour and egg recipe.

Ravioli hold up well in the freezer (4 to 6 weeks). Use a cookie sheet that will fit into your freezer. Lay out the cut and sealed ravioli on the sheet to dry. Turn them over after 10 minutes. Put the cookie sheet into the freezer. Within 2 hours they will be frozen. Put the frozen ravioli into small plastic bags in serving portions or put them all in a large plastic freezer bag, seal the bag, and put it back into the freezer.

When cooking frozen ravioli, take them directly from the freezer to the boiling water. Do not allow them to thaw. Frozen ravioli take 2 to 3 minutes more to cook than freshly made ravioli.

The consistency and thinness of the dough determine the number of ravioli a basic dough recipe will yield. For example, using Method Two (rolling the dough through a pasta machine and using a ravioli form) I have made 41 ravioli, 2 inches by 2 inches, from a recipe that calls for 2 eggs and 1½ cups of flour. I used every bit of dough and reworked the scraps of dough pulled away from the ravioli form. If you are making ravioli for the first time, you can easily count on 24 to 30 (2 inches by 2 inches) from a 2-egg dough recipe. As you gain experience the number will increase, especially if you use Method Two.

If you are not using a pasta machine to thin out the dough, the yield will be smaller as it is difficult to get the dough as thin using a rolling pin.

In the ravioli recipes that follow, the quantities for the filling will make between 24 and 32 ravioli squares, 2 inches by 2 inches—it all depends on the method used and the amount of filling in each ravioli. Also, no portions or number of servings are given, as appetites vary. You know your family and friends better than I do. My advice is to make enough; you can always freeze them if you have made too many. (Don't freeze them after they have been cooked.)

Ravioli with Ricotta and Sausage

Pasta
2 extra-large eggs
1½ cups unbleached
  flour

Filling
1½ cups ricotta
  cheese, well drained
½ cup grated
  mozzarella cheese
½ cup grated
  Parmesan cheese
1 tablespoon finely
  chopped parsley
1 egg
⅛ teaspoon freshly
  grated nutmeg
Salt and pepper to
  taste

Sauce
¼ cup chopped carrots
¼ cup chopped onions
¼ cup chopped celery
4 tablespoons
  unsalted butter
1 can (28 ounces)
  Italian-style plum
  tomatoes
½ pound Italian
  sausage, casing
  removed
⅓ cup olive oil
2 tablespoons finely
  chopped parsley
Salt
Freshly ground
  pepper

Order of Preparation:
Make the filling and
  refrigerate.
Make the sauce.
Make the pasta
  dough.
Make and cook the
  ravioli.

1   To make the filling: Combine all the ingredients in a mixing bowl. Mix thoroughly and beat the mixture until smooth.

2   To make the sauce: Over medium heat, cook the carrots, onions, and celery in the butter until they are slightly softened. Add the tomatoes and their juice, breaking up the tomatoes with a wooden spoon or spatula. Remove from the heat.

In a separate pan, cook the sausage in the oil, breaking up any large lumps. When the sausage is fully cooked, drain off any excess fat. Set aside.

Pass the tomato sauce through a food mill into a bowl. Add this puree to the pan with the sausage. Add the finely chopped parsley. Taste and add salt if necessary. Add the pepper. Bring the sauce to a slow boil over medium heat. Reduce the heat to maintain a slow simmer. Cook for 30 to 40 minutes, stirring occasionally.

3   While the sauce is cooking, make the pasta dough with the extra-large eggs and the flour, following the basic recipe.

4   Fill and seal the ravioli. Cook the ravioli in plenty of boiling salted water. When the ravioli are done, put them into a heated serving dish and dress with the sauce. Serve with additional Parmesan cheese.

After the ravioli have been dressed with the sauce, they can be kept in a warm oven for 15 to 20 minutes.

Ravioli with Ricotta, Butter, and Parmesan

Pasta
2 extra-large eggs
1½ cups unbleached
  flour

Filling
1½ cups ricotta
  cheese, well drained
½ 10-ounce package
  frozen chopped
  spinach, squeezed
  dry, and finely
  chopped
⅓ cup grated
  Parmesan cheese
1 egg
Salt
Pepper

Sauce
¼ pound unsalted
  butter, melted
1 cup freshly grated
  Parmesan cheese
Freshly ground white
  pepper

Order of Preparation:
Make the filling and
  refrigerate.
Make the pasta
  dough.
Make the ravioli.
Dress with the sauce.

1   To make the filling: Combine all the filling ingredients in a mixing bowl. Mix thoroughly. Lightly beat the mixture until smooth. Taste and add salt if necessary. Add pepper to taste.

2   Make the pasta dough with the extra-large eggs and the flour, following the basic recipe.

3   Fill and seal the ravioli. Cook the ravioli in plenty of boiling salted water.

4   When the ravioli are done, spread a layer in a heated serving dish. Pour some of the melted butter over them and sprinkle on some of the grated Parmesan. Add another layer of ravioli, butter, cheese, etc. Top with butter and cheese and pepper. Bake in a preheated 375° F. oven for 15 minutes. Serve immediately.

Another sauce that can be used for this dish is a light béchamel. Follow the same procedure for dressing with the butter and Parmesan. Top with béchamel and sprinkle grated Parmesan on top. Bake in the oven until the top is lightly browned.

If fresh sage is available, mix it with the butter while it is melting.

Ravioli with Chicken

Pasta
2 extra-large eggs
1½ cups of unbleached flour

Filling
½ 10-ounce frozen chopped spinach, cooked, squeezed dry, and finely chopped
1½ cups chicken, cooked, skinned, and finely chopped
2–3 slices mortadella, finely chopped
1 egg
¼ cup grated Parmesan cheese
Chicken broth
Salt
Pepper

Sauce
4 tablespoons unsalted butter
2 cups heavy cream
¼ cup grated Parmesan cheese
⅛ teaspoon freshly grated nutmeg
Freshly ground white pepper

Order of Preparation:
Make the filling and refrigerate.
Make the pasta dough and the ravioli.
Make the sauce and cook the ravioli.

1   To make the filling: Combine the filling ingredients through the Parmesan in a mixing bowl and blend thoroughly. If the mixture is dry and too stiff, add some chicken broth to obtain a creamy consistency. Taste and add salt if necessary. Add pepper to taste. (See note.)

2   Make the pasta dough and fill and seal the ravioli.

3   To make the sauce: Use a pan large enough to hold the cooked ravioli (a 10- to 12-inch sauté pan). Over medium heat melt the butter but do not let it brown. Add the cream, stir thoroughly, and reduce slightly. The sauce can be set aside at this point until the ravioli are cooked. When the ravioli are cooked, add them to the cream and butter sauce. Turn the heat to medium. Add the Parmesan, the grated nutmeg, and the pepper. Gently toss and coat the ravioli with the sauce for 2 to 3 minutes as the sauce thickens slightly.

4   Serve at once on individual serving plates or in a heated oval serving dish.

To avoid all the chopping, the filling can be made in a food processor. Put all the ingredients, except the chicken broth, salt, and pepper, into the processor fitted with the steel blade. Pulse 2 or 3 times in 4- to 5-second bursts. Scrape down the sides of the work bowl between pulses. Don't make the mixture too pasty or homogenized. You do not want to lose the identity of the ingredients. Transfer the mixture to a mixing bowl. Add the chicken broth if necessary. Mix thoroughly. Taste and add salt if necessary. Add pepper to taste.

Ravioli with Beef and Veal

Pasta
2 extra-large eggs
1½ cups unbleached flour

Filling
½ pound ground chuck
¼ pound ground veal

3 tablespoons olive oil
½ cup dry white wine
1 egg
1 tablespoon finely chopped parsley
¼ cup grated Parmesan cheese
Salt
Pepper

Sauce
½ cup chopped onions
1 tablespoon unsalted butter
2 tablespoons olive oil
2 cloves garlic, peeled, and put through a garlic press
1 can (28 ounces) Italian-style plum tomatoes
2 teaspoons basil
2 teaspoons oregano
Salt

Order of Preparation:
Make the filling and refrigerate.
Make the sauce.
Make the pasta dough and the ravioli.
Cook the ravioli.

1 To make the filling: Over medium heat, cook the ground chuck and the ground veal in the olive oil until no traces of red are left in the meats. Scrape the bottom of the pan with a wooden spatula. Break up any large pieces of meat. Turn up the heat. Add the wine and cook until the wine has evaporated. Take the pan off the heat and let the mixture cool. Put the cooked meats in a mixing bowl. Add the egg, parsley, and grated Parmesan. Mix thoroughly and vigorously. Taste and add salt if necessary. Add pepper to taste. Refrigerate while you make the sauce.

2 To make the sauce: Over medium heat, cook the onions in the butter and oil until they are softened. Add the garlic. Stir and cook for about 1 minute (do not overcook the onions). Add the tomatoes through a food mill to the pan. Add the basil and oregano. Bring the sauce to a slow boil. Turn down the heat to maintain a slow, steady simmer. Cook for 30 minutes. Taste and add salt if necessary.

3 Make the pasta dough and fill and seal the ravioli.

4 Cook the ravioli in plenty of boiling salted water.

5 When the ravioli are done, put them into a heated oval or deep serving dish. Dress with the hot sauce. Serve additional sauce and grated Parmesan on the side.

After the ravioli have been dressed with the sauce they can be kept in a warm oven for 10 to 15 minutes.

Cavatelli with Tomato Sauce

In some locales this pasta is also known as gnocchi or seashells. The rolling and forming of the pasta is not done for aesthetic reasons; the ridges and the small pockets in the cavatelli help to pick up and hold the sauce.

Pasta
2 cups unbleached flour
¾ tablespoon vegetable oil or melted vegetable shortening
½ cup or more hot water
1 teaspoon baking powder

2 tablespoons olive oil
1 can (28 ounces) Italian-style plum tomatoes
2 tablespoons tomato paste
2 tablespoons finely chopped parsley
2 teaspoons oregano
Salt to taste

Sauce
1 clove garlic, peeled and put through a garlic press

Order of Preparation:
Make the sauce.
Make the pasta.
Cook the pasta.

Serves 4 as a first course or side dish

1 To make the sauce: Use a nonaluminum 2- to 3-quart sauté pan or saucepan. Over medium heat sauté the garlic in the oil for about 2 minutes. Add the tomatoes through a food mill. Add the tomato paste and mix thoroughly. Add the parsley and the oregano. Bring the sauce to a slow boil. Turn down the heat. Keep the sauce at a slow simmer (small bubbles). Simmer for 30 to 40 minutes. Taste and add salt if necessary.

2 To make the pasta: Use a fairly large mixing bowl. Put the flour into the bowl. Add the shortening.

3   Add the hot water and mix with your
    hands for about 2 minutes.

4   Add the baking powder.

5   Mix thoroughly with your hands until the
    dough comes together in a ball. At this
    point, if the dough feels stiff, add a bit
    more hot water. The dough should be quite
    soft and a bit spongy.

6   Take the dough out of the bowl and knead
    for 4 to 5 minutes as instructed in the
    beginning of the book. The dough should
    look like this.

7   Cut a piece of the dough about the size of a
    plum off the ball and keep the rest covered
    with a towel. Stretch and roll this piece
    between your hands to form a sausagelike
    shape.

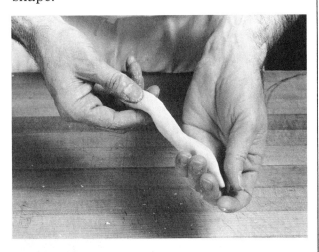

8   Place the dough on the counter and, with
    the lightest amount of pressure, roll your
    hands over the dough to stretch and thin it
    out. Continue until you have used all the
    dough.

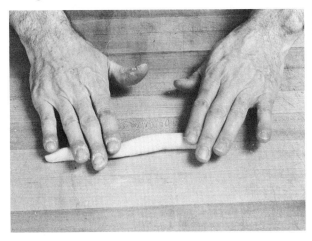

9   This is how the pieces will look, ready for cutting and rolling.

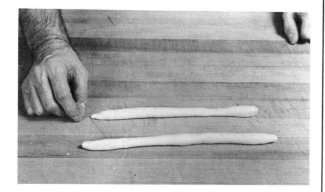

10   Cut the pasta cylinders into small pieces. Note the soft consistency of the dough.

11   Roll the pieces down over the tines of a fork, with some pressure, to form the cavatelli. The pasta is now ready for cooking.

12   If you are lucky enough to have a cavatelli machine, the work moves along faster. Feed the tube of dough between the rollers while turning the handle.

13   The machine forms and cuts the cavatelli, ready for the boiling water.

14   Cook the cavatelli in plenty of boiling salted water for about 4 minutes. Test with your teeth. They should be cooked through but offer a little resistance to the teeth. Because these are made without eggs, the consistency is different than that of pasta made with eggs.

15   When the cavatelli are cooked, drain well. Put them into a large serving bowl. Pour the sauce into the bowl. Mix well. Serve with additional sauce and grated Parmesan cheese.

Basic Cannelloni

Various sauces and fillings can be used with cannelloni. Below are the basic directions for preparing these stuffed rolls of pasta.

Pasta
2 extra-large eggs
1½ cups unbleached
   flour

Filling and Sauce
Filling and sauce
   from *Ravioli with*
   Beef and Veal

or
Filling and sauce
   from *Ravioli with*
   Ricotta and Sausage
or
Filling from *Ravioli*
   with Chicken and a
   light béchamel
   sauce or the sauce
   from *Ravioli with*
   Beef and Veal

Serves 6 as a first course or side dish

1   Follow the basic pasta dough recipe. Roll out the dough as thinly as possible. If using a pasta machine, stop at the next-to-last setting of the rollers.

2   Cut the sheet of pasta dough into rectangles about 3 inches by 4 inches. Cut 1 piece to that size and use it as a guide to cut the others. You will get about 8 rectangular pieces, 3 inches by 4 inches, from a sheet of dough that is 18 inches long and 6 inches wide; this is the standard width if you are using an Atlas or Imperia pasta machine.

3   Here are the pieces of dough ready for the boiling water. These pieces are slightly larger than the size recommended above. After cooking they will increase in size and the result will be 2 cannelloni from each piece of dough.

Do not allow the pieces to dry for more than 10 minutes before cooking.

4   Drop the pieces of dough, a few at a time, into a large pot of boiling salted water. About 2 minutes is enough cooking time as the pasta will have additional cooking time in the oven.

5   Have a bowl of cold water ready to receive the cooked pasta. Scoop the cannelloni out and lower into the cold water.

6   Quickly separate the pieces with your hands while the next batch is cooking.

7   Lay out the pieces on a clean towel that has been dampened and wrung dry.

8   Pat the top dry with another clean towel or paper towels. Let the pieces of pasta sit for about 30 minutes.

9   Lay the filling across the cooked pasta, slightly off center toward your body.

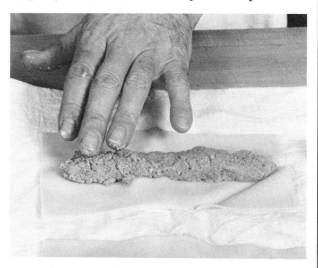

10 Roll the pasta around the filling away from you.

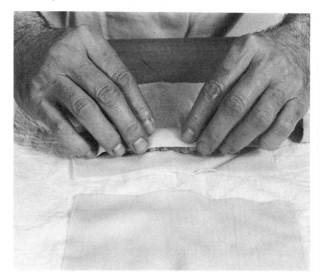

11 Place the cannelloni in a well-buttered baking dish. Dress with the sauce and bake in a preheated 400° F. oven for 15 to 20 minutes.

You will note that the cooked pasta is larger in size than the uncooked. The dough will expand by an inch or more in the cooking. In this sequence, I cut each cannelloni into 2 equal pieces after they were rolled—note the size of the cannelloni in the baking dish compared to the size during the rolling.

Basic Tortellini

There is a great deal of controversy over the origin of these little dumplings; the cities of Modena and Bologna in northern Italy have both claimed title to their "birth." Regardless of the outcome of this "battle of the tortellini," the winners will be your family and guests. They are worth the extra time necessary to make them. Don't you want to find out what the fuss is all about?

Like ravioli and cannelloni, tortellini can be stuffed and sauced with a variety of savory concoctions. The basic recipe follows.

Pasta	*Filling and Sauce*
2 extra-large eggs	Filling and sauce
1½ cups unbleached	from *Ravioli with*
flour	*Ricotta and Sausage*
	or
	Filling and sauce
	from *Ravioli with*
	Chicken

Serves 4 to 6 (60 to 64 tortellini)

1 Make the pasta dough following the basic recipe. If you are using a pasta machine, stop at the next-to-last setting on the rollers. If rolling by hand, roll the dough as thin as possible. Follow the basic technique described at the beginning of the book.

Keep the dough from drying out by covering ½ with a slightly damp towel while rolling the other ½. Keeping the dough soft facilitates the sealing of the edges. Also, adding a tablespoon of olive oil or milk to the basic recipe helps soften the dough for easier sealing.

2 Cut circular disks about 2 inches in diameter from the sheet of dough using a round cutter or a glass. Put a small amount of filling in the center of each disk. Try 1 or 2 at the start to get a feel for the right amount of filling to use. Once you've got it, you've got it.

3 Don't let the dough dry too much as it makes it harder to seal the edges. To make the sealing easier, dip your finger into a glass of warm water and wet the edge nearest you.

4 Fold the dough toward you until the two edges almost meet. Press down firmly along the rounded edge to seal in the filling.

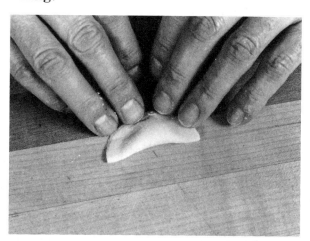

5 Hold the filled and sealed piece of dough between your thumb and index finger.

6 Fold it around your finger and bring the two ends together.

7 Press the two ends together to seal (my right hand); fold the top edge down (my left hand).

8 Follow the same procedure as for cooking ravioli, page 72.

Set the tortellini on a clean towel or a cookie sheet as you make them. They can be cooked at once or allowed to dry for 30 to 40 minutes (turn them once or twice so they dry evenly). If they are to be cooked later in the day, they should be refrigerated. The tortellini can be frozen and bagged as shown in the ravioli section.

Basic Cappelletti

Cappelletti are quite similar to tortellini, but instead of cutting a round disk, cut 2-inch squares of dough. Various sauces and fillings can be used with them. Below are basic directions for preparing cappelletti.

Pasta	*Filling and Sauce*
See *Basic Pasta Dough* (Chapter 3)	Filling and sauce from *Ravioli with Chicken*
	or
	Filling and sauce from *Ravioli with Beef and Veal*

The quantity of eggs and flour for making the dough and the handling and storing procedures are the same as for the tortellini recipe, pages 81–82.

Serves 4 to 6 (60 to 64 cappelletti)

1   Cut the squares from the thinned out dough. Place the filling (slightly larger than a pea) in the center. Dip your finger into a glass of warm water and wet 2 sides of the square.

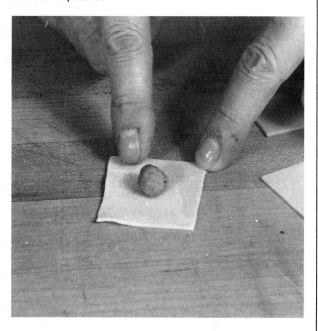

2   Fold the dough over onto the moistened edges (I turned the dough around to make it easier for you to see the method) until the 2 points almost meet.

3   Press down along the edges to seal the dough.

4   Put the cappelletti between your thumb and index finger and with your other hand press the 2 edges together firmly (my right hand). Pull back the peak slightly (the pointed ends just above my left thumb).

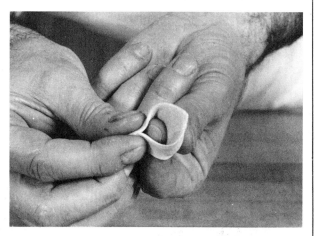

5   Follow the same procedure as for cooking ravioli, page 72.

Semolina Gnocchi

1 quart milk
1 cup semolina
¼ cup melted unsalted
   butter
¼ cup grated
   Parmesan cheese
3 egg yolks, lightly
   beaten

Salt
1 teaspoon nutmeg
2 tablespoons melted
   unsalted butter
¼ cup grated
   Parmesan cheese

Serves 4 as a first course or side dish

1   Bring the milk to a boil over medium heat.
    Add the semolina in a steady stream,
    stirring constantly. Keep stirring and
    cooking for about 6 minutes until the
    mixture thickens. Watch the heat. If the
    semolina starts to stick to the bottom of
    the pan, take it off the heat for a minute
    and reduce the heat to medium.

2   This is how the mixture will look when it
    is nearly done. Notice how it comes away
    from the side of the pan.

3   Add the ¼ cup melted butter and keep
    stirring.

4   Add the ¼ cup grated Parmesan and mix
    thoroughly. Watch the heat; it should not
    be too high at this point.

5   Add the lightly beaten egg yolks. At this
    point remove the pan from the heat and
    beat the mixture rapidly and vigorously to
    prevent the eggs from curdling.

6 Add the salt and the nutmeg. Mix thoroughly. Taste and add more salt if necessary. Be careful; the mixture will be very hot.

7 Dampen a jelly roll pan or baking sheet with water. Pour the gnocchi onto the sheet.

8 Smooth it out with a spatula to approximately ¼-inch thick. Use a pan that is 11 by 14 inches if you have one. Put the pan in the refrigerator for at least 1 hour to let the gnocchi firm up. You can make the dish a day ahead up to this point.

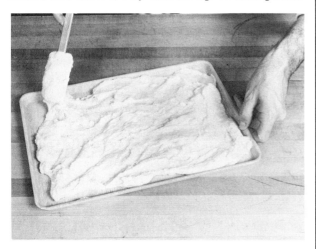

9 Butter an ovenproof serving dish.

10 Using a glass or a cutter approximately 1½ inches in diameter, cut the gnocchi into rounds.

11 This picture gives you a relative idea of the thickness. Lift out the pieces; continue until all are cut.

12 Lay them in the buttered dish with a slight overlap.

13 Pour the 2 tablespoons of melted butter over the gnocchi.

14 Sprinkle ¼ cup of freshly grated Parmesan cheese on top. Bake in a preheated 400° F. oven for 15 to 20 minutes until the cheese has browned lightly.

15 The finished dish. Serve at once.

If you are careful about how closely you cut out the circles the yield can be increased by 25 percent. Or, you can gather up the "holes" into a ball; flatten it out with a rolling pin or between your hands and make even more gnocchi.

Spinach Gnocchi

Pasta
1 cup or more unbleached flour
1 extra-large egg
1 10-ounce package frozen chopped spinach, cooked, well drained, and finely chopped
6 ounces ricotta cheese

Sauce
Red sauce (see *Lasagna with Chicken*, page 60 or *Cavatelli with Tomato Sauce*, page 76)

Serves 6 to 8 as a first course or side dish

1 Put the flour into a mixing bowl and add the egg.

2 Add the chopped spinach to the bowl. Preparation for this dish is made much easier if you get all the water out of the spinach. Cook the spinach well ahead of time. Squeeze out the water between your hands, then spread the spinach out on a small chopping board. Or, sauté it lightly to evaporate the water.

3 Add the ricotta cheese. Mix it all together very thoroughly to form a ball of dough.

4 Take the dough out of the mixing bowl and start kneading. Add flour as you knead as the dough will still be quite sticky.

5 Knead vigorously for about 8 to 10 minutes, adding more flour as needed. This is how it should look when it is ready.

6 Chop off small pieces with a dough scraper or knife.

7   Roll it out into small tubes about the size of bread sticks. Use the tips of your fingers, exerting a slight amount of pressure.

8   Cut the tubes into small squares.

9   Press down on the small squares with your thumb to make small hollows in the center.

10   Cook the gnocchi in plenty of boiling salted water, a few at a time. When they surface they are done. Transfer them at once with a slotted strainer to a serving dish. Use the red sauce of your choice.

Another method for serving is to put all the cooked gnocchi in an ovenproof dish. Add the sauce. Sprinkle Parmesan cheese on top; bake in a preheated 400° F. oven for about 15 minutes.

The dough can be made up to a day ahead, wrapped in plastic and foil, and refrigerated.

8

Pasta secche (dried pasta) is a relatively good substitute for Pasta all'uovo (freshly made flour-and-egg pasta), provided it is imported. The recipes on the following pages are offered if you have neither the time nor the inclination to make your own pasta.

It is strongly recommended that you use only a good brand of imported pasta, DeCecco or Agnesi brands being two of the best. Every package of Agnesi or DeCecco pasta states: this macaroni, made of the best quality of durum wheat, constitutes an excellent food exquisite in flavor—*made of pure semolina*. The key words are *pure semolina*. This is what makes these imported pastas (and others) far superior to a dried pasta made without it. It is superior in that it maintains a sincerity in the cooking that stays with you throughout the eating. Dried pasta made without semolina has a tendency to become soft and gummy in the cooking no matter how careful you are.

I have done tests using the imported pasta—cooking a full pound, eating half, storing the rest in the refrigerator. The next day I would pass some through a hot water bath for a minute or so; the consistency held and the pasta did not get mushy. This does not work with dried pasta made without semolina.

Consider, too, the wide variety of pasta available of the dried, imported type—upward of eighty (and more on the way). This is part of the excitement of dried pasta—fusilli, lumache, penne, ziti, rigatoni, and the list goes on. Each shape embraces the sauce in its own special way, making each dish taste a bit different. Try the same sauce on two different types of pasta—it tastes different. This lies, I believe, in the way the teeth and the pasta play out their individual performances.

The cares and worries of the day seem to disappear when one is eating pasta; the very attention to the detail of the eating does not allow for other concerns. This is not an original thought on my part, but one that comes from another serious pasta eater.

Some Tips on Using Pasta Secche

1   Always cook the pasta in plenty of boiling salted water—at least 4 to 5 quarts to the pound.

2   Make sure the water is boiling vigorously before adding the salt.

3   When you add the pasta, add it in batches to help keep the water at the boiling point.

4   Don't break the pasta (spaghetti and linguine types) in half before adding it to the water. This destroys the character of the pasta.

5   After adding the pasta to the boiling water, give it a good stir, cover the pot, bring the water back to a boil, and remove the cover. Stir it 3 or 4 times during the cooking.

6 Dried pasta takes longer to cook than freshly made pasta—usually 8 to 12 minutes, depending on the type and the thinness. Let your teeth be the judge—no overcooking, please.

7 There is no need to add oil to the water in which the pasta is to be cooked. This only makes the pasta slippery and serves no purpose. If the water is at a full boil and you give it a good stir at the beginning and a few stirs in between, you can save the oil for a nice salad.

8 Never rinse off the cooked pasta with cold water (except in specified recipes). This only serves to run up your water bill and takes away from the good taste of the pasta.

9 The yields given are really only estimates. It is possible that 1 pound of pasta could serve 8; it depends on the appetite, the age, and the type of people being served. A serious teenaged pasta eater might easily handle 2 serving portions. Let your experience and the situation be your guide.

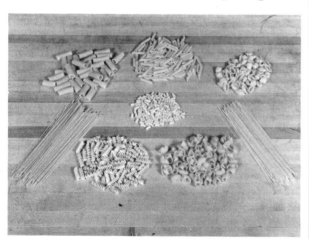

Linguine with White Clam Sauce

Pasta
1 pound linguine

Sauce
36 cherrystone or littleneck clams, scrubbed (see note **page 92**)
½ cup water

2 cloves garlic, sliced
2 tablespoons olive oil
1½–2 cups clam juice
2 tablespoons finely chopped parsley
2 teaspoons thyme
Pepper
Salt

Serves 4 as a main course

1 Scrub the clams well with a stiff-bristled brush. Put the water and the clams into a large pot set over high heat. Cover the pot.

2 Steam the clams until the shells open. This will take between 7 and 10 minutes, depending on the size of the clams. Give the clams a good stirring halfway through the steaming process. Remove the pot from the heat at once.

3 Put a colander, lined with 2 layers of a fine-meshed cheesecloth, into a large bowl. Pour the clams and the juice into the colander. This will strain the clam juice and get rid of any sand you may have missed in the scrubbing process. Measure out about 2 cups of the clam juice from the bowl.

4 Remove the clams from their shells and put clams into a separate bowl. Discard any clams that did not open during the steaming. Set the clams aside. Reserve 8 to 10 clam shells for decoration.

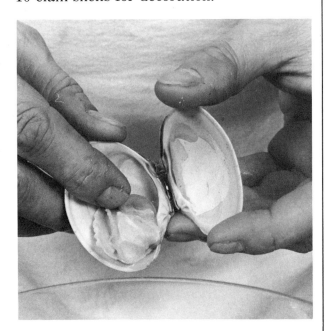

5 Prepare the clam sauce. In a saucepan set over medium heat, sauté the garlic in the oil until it is lightly browned. Discard the garlic.

6 Add the strained clam juice to the pan. Turn down the heat a bit. (If using canned minced clams, pour the juice from the can into the pan; reserve the clams.)

7 Add the chopped parsley and the thyme. Stir well. Keep the sauce warm over low heat. Add pepper to taste. Taste and add salt if necessary.

8 Put the cooked and well-drained linguine into a heated serving bowl.

9 Put the clams into the sauce for a very short time—less than a minute. If you leave the clams in the sauce too long, they will toughen.

10 Work quickly so the pasta does not cool. With a slotted spoon, remove the clams from the sauce and put on top of the pasta. Pour all the sauce over the pasta.

11 Place the reserved clam shells around the edge of the serving bowl. Serve at once.

For a richer taste add 2 tablespoons of unsalted butter to the cooked pasta just before adding the clams and the juice.

The linguine used in this recipe and those to follow is DeCecco brand. The package reads: N. 7—Lingue Di Passeri.

If fresh clams are not available, substitute 3 6½-ounce cans minced clams with juice. You will need to add some bottled clam juice (about 1 cup) to get 2 cups of juice. Follow the same procedure—add the chopped clams to the sauce at the very last.

Neapolitans use the larger clams for this dish. Baby clams, called vongole *in Italy, are excellent too. Increase the quantity to 48 if using the baby clams.*

Linguine with Red Clam Sauce

Pasta
1 pound linguine

Sauce
36 cherrystone clams
  (see note page 92)
½ cup water
2 cloves garlic,
  pressed
¼ cup olive oil

1–1½ cups clam juice
1 can (28 ounces)
  Italian-style plum
  tomatoes
1 tablespoon chopped
  parsley
Salt
Pepper

Serves 4 as a main course

1   Steam the clams open as described in the recipe for *Linguine with White Clam Sauce.* Take the clams out of their shells and chop them coarsely.

2   Put the garlic cloves through a garlic press into a sauté pan with the olive oil. Over medium heat, sauté the garlic for 2 minutes.

3   Add the clam juice from the fresh clams (see *Linguine with White Clam Sauce*) or the drained juice from the canned clams.

4   Pass the tomatoes through a food mill into the sauté pan. Stir well. Bring the sauce to a slow boil. Turn the heat down to maintain a steady simmer. Add the chopped parsley. Simmer for 45 minutes. Stir occasionally. Taste and add salt if necessary. Pepper to taste.

5   Put the cooked, well-drained linguine into a heated serving bowl.

6   Add the chopped clams (or canned minced clams) to the tomato sauce. Stir well. Let the clams just heat through, about 1 minute only.

7   Using a slotted spoon, put the clams into the center of the bowl. Pour the sauce around the inside edge of the bowl.

8   Your finished dish. Serve at once.

Don't use Parmesan cheese with either of the clam sauce recipes. The cheese will take away from the delicate flavor of the clams. The only complement needed for this dish is fresh Italian bread. If fresh clams are not available, substitute 3 6½-ounce cans minced clams. (Saltësea is a recommended brand.) A nice variation on this dish is to use fresh mussels with spinach fettuccine. Follow the same procedure with the mussels as for the clams.

Linguine with Scallops

Pasta
1 pound linguine

Sauce
1 clove garlic, pressed
2 tablespoons olive oil
1 cup clam juice
1 can (28 ounces) Italian-style plum tomatoes

2 teaspoons thyme
Salt

1 pound bay or sea scallops (see note below)

Serves 4 as a main course

1   To make the sauce: Put the clove of garlic through a garlic press into a sauté pan with the olive oil. Sauté the garlic for 2 minutes over medium heat. Scrape the bottom of the pan with a wooden spatula. Add the bottled clam juice (or fish stock, if you have any). Roughly chop the tomatoes in the can and add them to the pan, or pass the tomatoes through a food mill into the pan. Add the thyme. Stir well. Cook the sauce over low heat for 45 minutes, maintaining a slow steady simmer. Stir thoroughly every so often.

Start cooking the pasta about 10 minutes before the sauce is ready.

2   About 3 minutes before the pasta is done, add the scallops to the sauce. If using sea scallops, cut the larger ones into smaller pieces. Scallops cook very quickly. If you overcook them, they will toughen. Taste the sauce and add salt if necessary.

3   Put the cooked and well-drained pasta into a heated serving dish. Using a slotted spoon, put the scallops on top of the pasta.

4   Pour the sauce directly from the pan on top of the pasta.

5   The finished dish. Serve at once.

Do not use any cheese with this dish as it destroys the delicate balance of flavors.

An excellent substitute for the scallops is peeled and deveined shrimp. Follow the same procedure as for the scallops. The shrimp may take slightly longer to cook. Arrange some of the shrimp around the edge of the serving dish for a nice presentation.

Linguine with Anchovies

Pasta
1 pound linguine

Sauce
½ cup olive oil
¼ cup (2 ounces) anchovy fillets
2 cloves garlic, pressed

1 can (28 ounces) Italian-style plum tomatoes
2 tablespoons finely chopped parsley
Salt
Pepper

Serves 6 as a first course or side dish

1   Put the anchovies into a small bowl and wash them thoroughly to get rid of any salt.

Put the oil into a pan set over medium heat and add the anchovies.

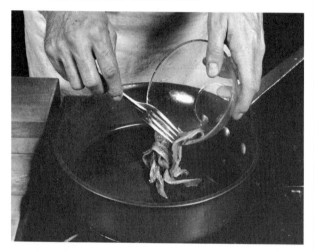

2   Using a fork, mash the anchovy fillets with the oil to form a paste.

3   Add the garlic, through a garlic press, to the pan. Turn down the heat a bit. Cook and stir for 2 minutes. Add the chopped parsley.

4   Pass the tomatoes through a food mill into the pan. Stir well, scraping the bottom of the pan with a wooden spatula. Cook the sauce for 45 minutes, maintaining a slow, steady simmer. If the sauce is not reducing and thickening, turn up the heat a bit. Taste and add salt if necessary. Add pepper to taste.

5 Put the cooked and well-drained pasta into a heated serving dish. Pour the sauce over the pasta. Reserve some sauce for passing at the table. Stir well. Serve at once.

Test the sauce for salt only toward the very end of the cooking as the anchovies may give off more salt during the simmering. If the sauce is excessively salty, add a bit of sugar to sweeten it. No cheese is necessary for this dish.

Lumache with Four Cheeses

Pasta
1 pound lumache grande (see note below)

Sauce
1 cup diced Fontina cheese
1 cup diced Bel Paese cheese
1 cup diced Gruyère cheese

1 cup grated Parmesan cheese
1 cup finely chopped prosciutto
1 pint heavy cream
1 egg yolk, beaten
Salt
Freshly ground white pepper

Serves 6 as a first course or side dish

1 Prepare the cheeses: Grate the Parmesan. Dice the others.

2 Over low heat, sauté the chopped prosciutto for 3 to 4 minutes. Do not let it brown. Do not use any oil or butter.

3 Add all the heavy cream to the pan. Scrape the bottom of the pan with a wooden spatula. Turn the heat to medium high and bring the cream to a slow boil.

4 Add all the cheese except the Parmesan to the cream. Stir constantly while the cheese is melting. Watch the heat. If the cream is bubbling too strongly, turn the heat down.

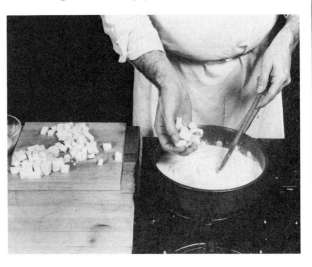

5   When all the diced cheeses are almost melted, add the Parmesan cheese. Keep stirring. You must make sure all the cheeses are blended together.

6   Add the egg yolk to the pan and mix it in quickly and thoroughly. When all the cheese has been blended together, test carefully for salt—the sauce will be very hot. Add the freshly ground white pepper.

7   Put the cooked and well-drained pasta into a heated serving dish.

8   Pour the sauce directly from the pan onto the pasta. Stir well with 2 large spoons to blend the sauce with the pasta.

9   Your finished dish. Serve at once.

The preparation of this dish moves along quickly; start cooking the pasta while the prosciutto is cooking. You can hold the preparation up to the point of adding the diced cheeses.

If lumache grande is not available, use any type of short, hollow pasta that will "grab" the cheese sauce.

Penne with Tomato and Ricotta

This is an extremely flavorful dish. By all means try to use pancetta. Many specialty Italian food stores carry this flavorful bacon. Carefully wrapped, it will last for 2 to 3 months in the refrigerator. If you can get some, keep it on hand, as it works well with many red sauces.

Pasta	½ cup pancetta or salt
1 pound penne	pork, chopped
	⅓ cup dry white wine
Sauce	1 can (28 ounces)
½ cup chopped onion	Italian-style plum
2 tablespoons olive oil	tomatoes
1 tablespoon unsalted	Salt and pepper
butter	1 cup ricotta cheese,
1 clove garlic, peeled	well drained
and put through a	½ cup grated
garlic press	Parmesan cheese

Serves 6 as a first course or side dish

1   In a sauté pan set over medium heat, sauté the onion in the oil and butter until it is soft but not limp.

2   Put the garlic through the press into the pan. Cook and stir for 2 minutes. Remove from the heat.

3   In a separate pan set over low heat, sauté the chopped pancetta until it renders most of its fat. Pancetta is a rolled, unsmoked Italian bacon as shown here. If pancetta is not available, use salt pork.

4   Add the cooked pancetta to the pan with the onion and garlic. Turn the heat to high.

5   Add the wine and cook until the wine has completely evaporated and all scent of wine is gone. Turn the heat to medium.

6   Pass the tomatoes through a food mill into the pan. Stir well. Bring the sauce to a slow boil, then turn down the heat to low to maintain a steady simmer. Simmer for 40 minutes. Salt and pepper to taste.

7   Ten to 12 minutes before the sauce is ready, cook the pasta in plenty of boiling salted water. Drain well. Put the cooked pasta into a heated serving bowl.

8   Pour the sauce over the pasta. Do not stir.

9   Spoon the ricotta, directly onto the hot sauce. Do not stir.

10   Add the grated Parmesan. Stir well to incorporate the cheese with the pasta.

11   The finished dish. Serve at once.

Penne with Broccoli

Pasta	Italian-style plum
1 pound penne	tomatoes
	1 tablespoon finely
Sauce	chopped parsley
2 cloves garlic, peeled	Salt
and put through a	Pepper
garlic press	1 large head broccoli
2 tablespoons olive oil	½ cup grated
2 can (28 ounces)	Parmesan cheese

Serves 6 as a first course or side dish

1   Prepare the sauce. Sauté the garlic in the oil over medium heat until it just starts to brown.

2   Pass the tomatoes through a food mill into the pan with the garlic. Stir thoroughly. Add the parsley. Bring the sauce to a slow boil. Turn the heat to low to maintain a steady simmer. Simmer for 30 minutes. Taste and add salt if necessary. Add pepper to taste.

3   While the sauce is simmering, prepare the broccoli. Wash it under cold running water. Cut off the stalk close to the head. Divide the head into flowerets. Cut the stalk into bite-sized pieces. Blanch the broccoli in a large pot of boiled salted water—first the stem pieces, about 3 minutes; then the flowerets. Eight minutes should be about the maximum cooking

time. When a knife pierces the stalk easily the broccoli is done. Don't overcook the broccoli—it should be on the firm side. Drain immediately and set aside.

4   Ten to 12 minutes before the sauce is ready, cook the pasta. Drain well and put the pasta into a heated serving dish.

5   Add the cooked broccoli to the pasta. Stir gently but thoroughly.

6   Pour the sauce over the pasta and the broccoli. Stir again.

7   Add the grated Parmesan. Stir once more. Serve at once.

If your timing is good, it is not necessary to keep the cooked broccoli warm. The sauce can cook a bit longer than the recommended 30 minutes, so if you start the broccoli a few minutes after you start the pasta cooking, everything should be ready about the same time. Work quickly to keep the dish hot.

Penne with Meat and Ham

Pasta
1 pound penne

Sauce
½ cup chopped onions
2 tablespoons olive oil
1 tablespoon unsalted
   butter
½ pound ground
   chuck
½ cup dry white wine

2 ounces prosciutto,
   chopped
1 can (28 ounces)
   Italian-style plum
   tomatoes
1 tablespoon finely
   chopped parsley
Salt
Pepper

½ cup freshly grated
   Parmesan cheese

Serves 6 as a first course or side dish

1 Over medium heat, sauté the onion in the oil and butter until they are slightly softened.

2 Add the ground chuck, crumbling it with your fingers. Cook until all traces of red are gone from the meat. Break up any large chunks with a spatula or fork.

3 Turn the heat to high and add the wine. Cook until the wine has completely evaporated (you will not detect any smell of alcohol).

4 Add the chopped prosciutto to the pan. Cook and stir for another 3 minutes. Turn the heat down to medium.

5 Pass the tomatoes through a food mill into the pan. Stir well. Add the chopped parsley. Cook the sauce for 1 hour, maintaining a slow simmer (occasional small bubbles). Taste and add salt if necessary. Add pepper to taste.

6 Put the cooked and well-drained pasta into a heated serving bowl.

7 Spoon the sauce onto the pasta. Reserve some sauce for passing at the table.

8 Sprinkle on the freshly grated Parmesan cheese. Stir thoroughly.

9 Your finished dish. Serve at once. Pass ½ cup or more extra Parmesan at the table.

Tubetti with Potatoes

Pasta
1 pound tubetti

Sauce
2 medium-sized red potatoes, peeled and diced
½ cup chopped onions
2 tablespoons olive oil
1 tablespoon unsalted butter
1 can (28 ounces) Italian-style plum tomatoes

½ cup beef broth
2 tablespoons finely chopped parsley
1 tablespoon oregano
Salt
Freshly ground pepper
½ cup peas
⅓ cup grated Parmesan cheese

Serves 6 as a first course or side dish

1 Prepare the potatoes: Peel, dice, and cook in a small amount of water until they are about half-cooked. Drain well and set aside.

2   In a sauté pan set over medium heat, sauté the onions in the oil and butter until soft but not limp.

3   Add the tomatoes to the pan, passing them through a food mill. Stir well.

4   Add the beef broth, parsley, and oregano. Turn up the heat. Bring the sauce to a slow boil. Turn the heat to low to maintain a steady simmer. Simmer for 30 minutes.

5   Ten to 12 minutes before the sauce is ready, start cooking the pasta and add the parboiled potatoes to the pan with the tomatoes. Stir well. Taste and add salt if necessary. Add the freshly ground pepper.

6   Add the peas. If using frozen directly from the package, allow 4 to 5 minutes for them to cook in the sauce. If they were cooked ahead of time, add them at the last minute.

7   Put the cooked and well-drained pasta into a heated serving bowl.

8   Pour the sauce directly into the bowl with the pasta.

9   Add the grated Parmesan. Mix well.

10 The finished dish. Serve at once with extra Parmesan.

This dish is easily converted to a soup course. Use ½ pound of pasta, 2 cans of tomatoes, 1 cup of beef broth. This will serve 8 people amply. For a more robust flavor, add some crushed red pepper flakes after the Parmesan.

If tubetti is not available, use a short, hollow pasta like ditalini.

Rigatoni with Tomato and Prosciutto

Pasta
1 pound rigatoni

Sauce
½ cup chopped onion
4 tablespoons unsalted butter
¼ pound mushrooms, sliced
4 ounces prosciutto, chopped

1 can (28 ounces) Italian-style plum tomatoes
1 tablespoon chopped parsley
Salt
Pepper

½ cup grated Parmesan cheese

Serves 6 as a first course or side dish

1   In a sauté pan set over medium heat, cook the onion in the butter until it is slightly softened.

2   Add the sliced mushrooms. Cook for 3 to 4 minutes until the mushrooms give up their moisture and are golden brown.

3   Add the chopped prosciutto. Cook and stir the mixture another 2 to 3 minutes.

4   Pass the tomatoes through a food mill into the pan. Turn up the heat. Add the chopped parsley. Bring the sauce to a slow boil. Turn the heat down to maintain a slow simmer. Taste and add salt if necessary. Add pepper to taste. Cook for 45 minutes, stirring occasionally.

5   Put the cooked and drained pasta into a heated serving bowl.

6   Pour the sauce over the pasta. Add the grated Parmesan. Mix well, but gently.

7   The finished dish. Serve at once.

Spaghetti with Classic Tomato Sauce

Pasta
1 pound spaghetti

Sauce
2 tablespoons finely chopped shallots
4 tablespoons unsalted butter
¼ cup diced carrots
¼ cup diced celery
1 can (28 ounces) Italian-style plum tomatoes

2 tablespoons dried oregano
Salt
Pepper
1 cup peas (fresh or frozen)

½ cup grated Parmesan cheese

Serves 6 as a first course or side dish

1   In a sauté pan set over medium heat, sauté the shallots in the butter until they are slightly softened.

2   Add the diced carrots and celery. Stir and cook for 3 to 4 minutes.

3   Pass the tomatoes through a food mill into the pan. As suggested earlier, if you do not have a food mill, roughly chop the tomatoes in the can with a knife and add the tomatoes and their juice to the pan. Add the dried oregano.

Bring the sauce to a slow boil. Turn down the heat and simmer the sauce for 1 hour, stirring occasionally. Taste and add salt if necessary. Add pepper to taste.

4   If using frozen peas, add them to the sauce 3 to 4 minutes before the pasta is done. If the peas are fresh or thawed, add them at the last minute.

5   Put the cooked and well-drained spaghetti into a heated serving bowl. An option, of course, is to fork the spaghetti onto individual serving plates.

6 Pour the sauce directly into the bowl with the cooked pasta. Stir well but gently.

7 Sprinkle ½ cup of freshly grated Parmesan cheese on top. Stir again. Serve at once.

My grandmother simplified this dish by using fresh tomatoes, peas, and basil, roughly chopped, from her garden. If you have fresh basil, do use it in place of dried oregano.

Spaghetti Carbonara

Pasta
1 pound spaghetti

Sauce
¼ pound pancetta or salt pork
1 tablespoon olive oil
3 eggs

½ cup freshly grated Parmesan cheese
Pepper
3 tablespoons unsalted butter, softened
Salt

Serves 6 as a first course or side dish

1 Roughly chop the pancetta or salt pork. In a sauté pan set over low heat, cook the pancetta very slowly in the oil. The idea is to render some of the fat from the pancetta. Once the pancetta has started to crisp up a bit, take the pan off the heat and set aside.

2 Meanwhile, break the eggs into a small bowl.

109

3 Add the freshly grated Parmesan to the eggs.

4 Combine the eggs and the cheese thoroughly. Add 2 or 3 grinds from a peppermill. Stir again.

5 Add the cooked and well-drained pasta to the pan with the pancetta. Be careful with the pasta—do not overcook as it will have some additional cooking in the sauté pan.

6 Turn the heat to medium low. Add the softened butter to the pan with the pasta.

7 Mix the pasta thoroughly. Stir up from the bottom of the pan to get all the flavoring from the pancetta. Watch the heat—it should not be too high.

8 Add the cheese-egg mixture. Work quickly at this point.

110

9 Take the pan off the heat. Stir quickly and thoroughly to incorporate all the ingredients. Taste and add salt if necessary. Add 2 or 3 more grinds with the peppermill.

10 Your finished dish, ready to serve. Serve at once.

Pesto

2 cups fresh basil
2 tablespoons pine nuts (pignoli)
1 tablespoon garlic, finely chopped
½–¾ cups olive oil (approximately)

½ cup freshly grated Parmesan cheese
Salt
Freshly ground pepper

Yields 1½ to 2 cups

Food Processor or Blender Method

1 Wash the basil; strip the leaves from the stems. Pat dry. Put the basil leaves, pine nuts, garlic, and olive oil in the processor (use the steel blade), or blender. Process until a smooth sauce is formed.

2 Transfer the sauce to a small mixing bowl. Add the Parmesan and mix thoroughly. Salt and pepper to taste. Control the consistency of the sauce by adding some of the hot water from the pot in which the pasta is cooked. The pesto should be the consistency of a tomato puree.

3 Cook the pasta in plenty of boiling salted water. Drain thoroughly and put into a serving bowl. Pour the pesto sauce over the pasta. Mix thoroughly. Serve at once.

Mortar and Pestle Method

1 Pound the washed and stripped basil leaves in a mortar with the pine nuts and the garlic. Slowly add the olive oil, continuing to mix thoroughly with the pestle to form a smooth paste. Add the cheese and combine thoroughly. Salt and pepper to taste.

2 Cook the pasta in plenty of boiling salted water. Drain thoroughly and put into a serving bowl. Pour the pesto sauce over the pasta. Mix thoroughly. Serve at once.

The balance of the ingredients for pesto sauce is critical but not unchangeable. The garlic can be altered to taste, as can the cheese. Using all Parmesan gives a milder flavor; a combination of Parmesan and Pecorino cheese gives a more pungent flavor to the pesto.

A pesto sauce has many uses: most commonly with trenette (a pasta slightly thicker than linguine) or linguine. I find pesto compatible with other pasta types such as lumache or penne. Pesto sauce swirled into minestrone soup is a tasty variation. A tablespoon in an egg salad adds an interesting taste.

113

The traditional pesto genovese is made with trenette and boiled potatoes. Cook the peeled and cubed potatoes in boiling water (one large potato for one pound of pasta) until just cooked—not soft. Add the boiled potatoes to the cooked pasta just before adding the pesto sauce. Mix thoroughly.

Because fresh basil is not available in many areas year-round it is advisable to freeze some pesto sauce for later use. Make the pesto as directed—except do not add the cheese. Put the sauce in small plastic storage containers and freeze. When ready to use put the sauce in a small saucepan over low heat. When the sauce is completely thawed add the cheese and mix thoroughly. Add a little of the hot pasta water if necessary to alter the consistency.

Tomato Sauce with Sausage

1 clove garlic, sliced	3 tablespoons grated
1 tablespoon olive oil	Parmesan cheese
1 small onion,	1 can (28 ounces)
chopped	Italian-style plum
½ pound sweet Italian	tomatoes
sausage	1 can (8 ounces)
1½ teaspoons fennel	tomato puree
seeds	Salt
1 teaspoon oregano	Pepper
1 teaspoon basil	
1 tablespoon finely	
chopped parsley	

Yields approximately 2 cups

1   Slice garlic vertically and sauté in oil over medium heat until golden. Add the onions and cook until softened.

2   Remove the sausage from the casing and crumble into the pan. Add the fennel. Cook and stir until the sausage is thoroughly cooked, breaking up any large chunks with a fork or spatula.

3   Drain the pan of any excess fat. Add the oregano, basil, parsley, cheese, plum tomatoes and their juices, and the tomato puree. Break up the plum tomatoes with a fork or spatula.

4   Bring the sauce to a slow boil. Turn the heat to low to maintain a slow, steady simmer. Simmer for 1 hour, stirring occasionally. Taste and add salt if necessary. Add pepper to taste.

This is an excellent sauce for any type of pasta: for eggplant parmigiana, for lasagna (double the amount of sausage), and a perfect topping for pizza (grate mozzarella cheese over the sauce after putting it on the pizza dough).

Raw Tomato Sauce

2 pounds fresh, ripe	3–4 sprigs finely
tomatoes, peeled,	chopped parsley
seeded, chopped	Salt
½ cup finely chopped	Pepper
onions	
1 clove finely chopped	
garlic	

1   Wash the tomatoes. Blanch, peel, and seed the tomatoes as shown on pages 6–7. Roughly chop the tomatoes in a mixing bowl.

2   Add the onions, garlic, and parsley. Add salt and freshly ground pepper to taste.

3   Cook the pasta and drain. Use a short tubular pasta such as penne or ziti.

4   Add the pasta to the bowl with the sauce. Mix thoroughly.

5   The finished dish. Serve at once.

This amount of sauce is adequate for ½ to ¾ pound of cooked pasta. If available, substitute ½ cup finely chopped fresh basil leaves for the parsley.

Tuna Sauce

½ cup olive oil
2 cloves garlic, put
   through a garlic
   press
1 can (28 ounces)
   Italian-style plum
   tomatoes

1 teaspoon thyme
1 can (7 ounces)
   water-packed tuna
Salt
Pepper

1   In a sauce pan set over medium heat, sauté
    the garlic in the oil for 1 to 2 minutes. Do
    not allow the garlic to burn.

2   Pass the tomatoes through a food mill into
    the saucepan.

3   Add the thyme. Simmer the sauce over
    low heat for 45 minutes, stirring often.

4   Remove from heat and add tuna. Stir
    thoroughly to blend the tuna with the
    sauce. Salt and pepper to taste.

*This is enough sauce for ¾ to 1 pound of
cooked pasta. The sauce goes well with
spaghetti or linguine.*

AGLIO E OLIO: A simple, quick sauce using oil and garlic. Soak two cloves of garlic, finely chopped, in an extra-virgin olive oil while the pasta is cooking. Pour the sauce over the cooked and drained pasta (usually spaghetti). Toss well. Serve at once.

AGNOLOTTI: A filled pasta dumpling similar to ravioli, usually with a meat filling.

ALL AMATRICIANA: A sauce made by sautéing onion and bacon in oil, adding fresh or canned tomatoes, simmered for 15 to 20 minutes; served with spaghetti and freshly grated Parmesan cheese.

ALLA MARINARA: Sauce combining tomatoes, garlic, oil, and oregano.

BIGOLI: Pasta made with whole wheat flour and eggs.

CAPELLI DI ANGELO: "Angel's Hair" pasta, very fine, very thin.

CAPELLINI: A thin, round, and long pasta that resembles fine strands of hair from which the name is derived.

CAPPELLETTI IN BRODO: Make the cappelletti ("little hats") using a meat filling, chicken, or a combination of ground veal and ground pork (see pages 82–83). The cappelletti

are then poached in a rich chicken broth. Serve in soup bowls with grated Parmesan on the side.

CARRATTIERA: A name for a sauce (translates to "cart style") using tuna in oil, garlic, meat sauce, and Parmesan cheese. Usually served with spaghetti.

CHITARRA: Used in the Abruzzi region. A chitarra is a wooden frame with tautly strung wire strings (hence the name *guitar*). Thin sheets of pasta dough are laid over the strings, and by passing a rolling pin over the dough thin strings of pasta are formed.

ORECCHIETTE: "Little ears." A pasta shaped somewhat like ears. A nice soup made with this pasta: Crush two cloves of garlic in a hot chicken broth. Cook the orecchiette in the boiling broth. Three to 4 minutes before the pasta is done add washed broccoli flowerets. Salt and pepper to taste. Serve in soup bowls with crusty Italian bread.

PASTA AL FORNO: Pasta that has been cooked and then baked in the oven (lasagna, for example).

PASTA ALL'UOVO: Flour and egg pasta, usually handmade, sometimes called casalinga or "in the manner of the house."

PASTA FATTA IN CASA: Homemade pasta.

PASTA IN BRODO: Pasta in broth, such as tortellini in brodo.

PASTA RIPIENA: Stuffed and cooked pasta normally made using handmade pasta.

PASTA SECCHE: Dried, factory-made pasta made from durum wheat and water.

PROSCIUTTO CRUDO (raw ham): An important ingredient in Italian cooking. Its delicate flavor allows for many uses, especially in pasta dishes.

RAGÙ: Meat sauce.

RIGATONI: Short, fairly large tubular pasta.

SEMOLINA: The coarsely milled heart of the durum wheat grain. Used in all top quality brands of dried packaged pasta and for making semolina gnocchi.

SUGO: Gravy or sauce.

Index